TRIM CARPENTRY PROJECTS

Chris Marshall

SHADY OAK PRESS

Trim Carpentry Projects

By Chris Marshall

CREDITS

Tom Carpenter
Creative Director

Jen Weaverling
Managing Editor

Wendy Holdman
Senior Book Designer

Greg Schweiters
Cover Design

Mark Johanson
Book Products Development Manager, Editor

Dan Cary
Book Production Editor

Chris Marshall
Author

Bill Nelson
Series Design, Art Direction and Production

Mark Macemon
Lead Photographer

Ralph Karlen
Photographer

Bruce Kieffer
Illustrator

Craig Claeys
Contributing Illustrator

Brad Classon, John Nadeau
Production Assistance

Rex Cauldwell
Electrical Consultant

ISBN 978-1-58159-363-1

© 2001 North American Membership Group

1 2 3 4 5 6 7 8 / 12 11 10 09 08

Printed in China

Distributed by:
Sterling Publishing Co., Inc.
387 Park Avenue South
New York, NY 10016-8810

For information about custom editions, special sales, premium and corporate purchases, please contact Sterling Special Sales Department at 800-805-5489 or specialsales@sterlingpublishing.com.

SHADY OAK PRESS

12301 Whitewater Drive
Minnetonka, MN 55343

Trim Carpentry Projects

Table of Contents

Introduction

Whether you live in a 1960s rambler or a turn-of-the-century Queen Anne, your home has trimwork. At the very least, windows and doors are trimmed with case moldings and the floors are fitted with base trim. If you live in an older home or one designed with more than the usual survey of moldings, your home's list of trimwork may include details like window and door cornices, crown molding, picture rail, chair rail or plate rail, and perhaps wainscot or coffered ceiling trim. Even the woodwork around a fireplace is created using trim carpentry skills. This is why generations of carpenters have spent their entire careers installing trim in homes.

But you don't need to be a professional trim carpenter to have success installing trim. Trim carpentry, as a general skill, is trickier than it might seem at first glance. But it is manageable, enjoyable and rewarding if you approach it with patience, the right tools and plenty of solid information. *Trim Carpentry Projects* offers the key to solving all the trim carpentry challenges you'll encounter when working on your home. Whether you are replacing windows and doors, building an addition, or just trying to update the look of your house, you'll find the information you need to do the job right in the pages of this book.

With more than 300 full-color photographs and illustrations accompanied by carefully written text, this comprehensive book covers a wide range of trim carpentry issues and projects. First off, we'll help you identify different moldings and their typical uses, select a trim scheme for your project and calculate how much molding you need to buy. For those instances where off-the-shelf moldings won't do, there's even a section on how to make your own molding for a truly custom look.

The following sections are devoted to in-depth coverage of the trim carpentry projects tackled most often: replacing windows and doors, installing window and door casing, and running baseboard trim. Each section provides useful information and succinct, step-by-step projects so you can follow along from beginning to end. Even if you are a novice trim carpenter, these sections will help you install and maintain the essential trimwork in your home with confidence.

The remainder of the book covers a number of more advanced, unusual or ambitious trim carpentry topics and projects. We show you how to jazz up a ceiling with crown moldings or built-up cornice treatments. If a truly dramatic ceiling effect is what you're after, consider adding a coffered ceiling to a dining room or a formal living area. We'll show you how. *Trim Carpentry Projects* also provides an extensive section on installing wainscot, including frame-and-panel varieties that you can design and build from scratch or install as a kit. You'll also find complete plans for building and installing a handsome fireplace surround that's sure to add warmth to a room.

Woven throughout the step-by-step projects in this book, you'll learn important skill-building techniques, such as how to cut cope joints, how to fit moldings against unsquare walls or sagging floors, and the correct procedures for making trim carpentry joints just like the professionals do. Learn the secrets for cutting and tweaking miter joints so they fit tightly every time. If you've ever scratched your head when faced with cutting a compound miter angle, we'll demonstrate how to cut them with a simple jig instead of complex mathematics.

We think this assortment of projects and related techniques will prompt you to pull *Trim Carpentry Projects* off the shelf again and again for help with any trim project that comes your way.

IMPORTANT NOTICE

For your safety, caution and good judgment should be used when following instructions described in this book. Take into consideration your level of skill and the safety precautions related to the tools and materials shown. Neither the publisher, Shady Oak Press, nor any of its affiliates can assume responsibility for any damage to property or persons as a result of the misuse of the information provided. Consult your local building department for information on permits, codes, regulations and laws that may apply to your project.

Well integrated and thoughtfully planned trim moldings can unite diverse colors and patterns into a rich and stylish ensemble. The chair rail seen here is linked stylistically to the other trim in the room, and also causes the impression of wainscot. Photo courtesy of Premdor Inc.

Trim Carpentry Basics

The quality of the trim moldings can utterly change a room—for better or for worse. There are many factors that affect trim "quality", from the type of materials used to the installation techniques to the finishing to the many design decisions that come into play throughout the trim carpentry process.

In this chapter, you'll learn the most basic facts about trim carpentry: what types are available, what their purpose is, what they're made of, and much more. You'll also get an overview of the tools and fasteners that are so important to doing neat trim work. Plus, you'll find several highly useful techniques showing you how to make custom trim moldings right in your shop. To start it off, you'll see some pretty pictures that clearly show the wonderful effects trim can have on a room.

An ornate fireplace mantel built using trim carpentry techniques is the focal point of any room—from a lavish drawing room to a basement family room. Photo courtesy of Premdor Inc.

A coffered ceiling can transform an ordinary room into a cathedral-like setting.

Arched head casing over a half-moon transom has a dynamic effect that's enhanced by fluting. Photo courtesy of Pella Corporation.

Even the simplest joints and plainest wood trim look neat and professional when installed with skill. Photo courtesy of Premdor Inc.

Shelf rail adds valuable display/storage to the walls in any home, and with a touch of Victorian nostalgia to boot.

Paint is a perfect finish for trim molding in a contemporary or even Country setting, softening the overall ambience. Photo courtesy of Premdor Inc.

Clever use of trim can trick the eye easily. Here, mitered molding frames join forces with chair rail and base shoe to generate the look and feel of wainscot. Photo courtesy of Premdor Inc.

Frame a fabulous view with fantastic trim. Here, the stool and cap moldings on the window casing interact nicely with the cornice and basemolding. Photo courtesy of Pella Corporation.

Corner blocks and fluting add depth and elegance to any case molding scheme. The effect is intensified by repetition in these multiple window bays. Photo courtesy of Pella Corporation.

For sheer richness of wood tones, nothing can compare with all-wood wainscot—especially when it's built and finished by hand, a piece at a time.

There are not many rules when it comes to trim design. Wainscot is normally installed between 32 and 42 inches above the floor. But here, the 7-foot-high wainscot panels are a successful throwback to older wall panel styles. Photo courtesy of Anderson Windows Inc.

Style has a place in trim carpentry. The oak window casing in this Art-and-crafts room is wrapped with mitered backbanding strips—a very popular and authentic treatment from that period. Photo courtesy of Pella Corporation.

Moldings for Trim Carpentry

Moldings, the raw materials of trim carpentry, are narrow strips of wood (or other materials) with a decorative shape, called a profile, cut along the entire length. The profile is best illustrated when the molding is viewed in cross section. Technically, if a molding has no profile it is simply called trim, but we'll use the terms interchangeably in this book. The particular molding or moldings you select for trimming a window, door or wall adds visual interest to the room and contributes to the warmth and character of the space. When carefully chosen and installed, moldings seem to "anchor" walls to floors, providing graceful transitions between walls and ceilings and neatly tying together the features of a room.

An architect or interior designer will tell you that the presence of moldings in our homes can be traced back to the designs of Greek and Roman architecture. Temples were adorned with elaborate columns, ornate roof cornices and decorative ceiling and wall treatments. Today, we mimic those temple elements in a much subdued form when we wrap a door or window with wood—only now our "columns" have become side casings and our "cornices" have evolved into crown or cove molding. Even the molding profiles we use—combinations of oval or elliptical curves and flat planes—are in some cases direct throwbacks to patterns developed by the Ancients. Of course, the forms of moldings you'll find in your local building center or lumberyard are also influenced by trends in contemporary architecture, modern machining methods and the demands of the building market in your area.

Aside from decoration, trim serves several important practical functions. Moldings hide the gaps formed between walls and floors, window frames and door jambs. Molding also protects what it covers from the ordinary wear and tear of life—dings, scuffs, scratches, dirt. Early forms of molding around windows and doors actually provided a weatherproofing function, keeping wind, rain and insects out. Now, trim also helps to hide a variety of building imperfections by creating the illusion of flatness and uniformity around sagging ceilings or irregular walls, or even a window or door that wasn't hung squarely in the first place.

You don't need to be an architect to choose trim molding for a project. It's really more a matter of making some practical decisions. This section will acquaint you with the major categories of molding that relate to trim carpentry, so you'll be able to distinguish a base molding from a back band and know which

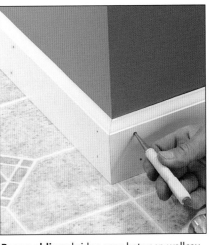

Basemoldings bridge gaps between wallcoverings and floors. They may or may not be equipped with base shoe or base cap.

goes where. You'll also need to make some decisions about what effect or style you're after when trimming the features of a room, along with issues of budget and time. Depending on your skill level and your project needs, you may decide to make molding in the shop from scratch or to have it custom-milled to your specifications, rather than buying it off the shelf.

Cornice moldings are decorative treatments that fit between walls and ceilings. Crown molding and sprung cove are common types.

Types of moldings. Most molding types have a specific intended use, but it is common for one type of molding, like base molding for example, to be used in ceiling applications or even to surround doors and windows. For the purposes of identification, here are the major types of interior trim molding and their typical applications.

Cornice (ceiling) moldings. Moldings that hide the corner formed by a ceiling and its adjacent walls can technically be lumped into a category called *cornice moldings.* The term cornice also refers to the product formed by joining a number of ceiling moldings together on a ceiling for a more dramatic effect. Common cornice moldings are crown, cove and bed moldings. Crown and bed moldings come in a range of widths and face profiles, but crown generally has a more elaborate and ornamental face and is wider than bed molding. Cove molding, unlike either crown or bed molding, has a simple concave profile. Rather than laying flat against the wall or ceiling, crown, bed and some cove moldings are known as *sprung molding*—that is, they tip outward from the walls at angles ranging from 32° to 45°. The molding itself is relatively thin, but both long edges are bevel-cut to meet the wall and ceiling, leaving a triangular gap behind the molding. Sprung molding is nailed to both the wall and ceiling, or to scraps of backing attached to the

Case moldings are used to conceal gaps between doors and windows and the rough opening frames that surround them.

wall. The gap formed behind sprung molding helps it conform to irregularities in the wall or ceiling. Smaller dimension cove molding has square edges, rather than beveled edges, so it fits all the way into the corner.

Basemolding. Basemolding, also called *baseboard* or simply *base,* is fastened to the bottoms of walls to hide ragged edges of the wall sheathing and cover gaps between the walls and floor. Ranging in width from 2¼ in. to more than 3 in., base molding generally is flat across most of its width, but has a decorative bead, ogee curve or gradual tapered roundover along the top edge. Depending upon the style, baseboard may consist of a single strip of molding all around the room or it may be combined with *base cap* molding, *quarter-round* or *base shoe* to create a more substantial, built-up look. Base cap is thin, flexible molding less than 1¼ in. wide, with a decorative profile along the face edge. It is attached to the top of flat-edged basemolding to introduce visual interest and help conceal gaps between the wider basemolding and the wall. Quarter-round and base shoe can be used alone as basemolding or nailed along the joint between wider basemolding and the floor to hide gaps. In cross-section, quarter-round actually is a quarter circle, while base shoe is narrower and elongated with a more gradual top curvature.

Case moldings (*or casings*) include the broad category of trim that frames door and window jambs on the sides and top, as well as the bottom of the window jamb on windows that aren't outfitted with a stool and apron. Profiles for case moldings vary widely, from simple flat faces with rounded edges to tapered "clamshell" shapes to elaborate convex and concave curves, beads and delicate reveals. Premilled casing varies in width from 2¼ in. to more than 3 in., but custom-milled or shop-made casing can go much wider. A portion of the back face of most manufactured case molding is recessed slightly so the molding can conform to uneven surfaces between walls and window or door jambs for a tighter fit. Aside from ornamentation, casing also functions to strengthen jamb and wall connections because the molding is nailed to both the jamb and the surrounding wall framing.

Cap moldings. The top, exposed edges of wall treatments like wainscot or the end grain of door head casings aren't desirable to see. So they're usually covered with *cap moldings* (also called *wainscot moldings*). Cap molding are milled with a rabbet groove that fits over and covers the top edges of the paneling, giving it a finished look. Visually, the molding makes the paneling appear to be on the same plane as the wall surface. Another form of cap molding, called backband (See page 68), wraps around the outer edges of window and door casings to make the casing look thicker than it actually is. The extra width provides a way for other moldings, like baseboard or chair rail, to butt against doors and windows and create a pleasing reveal. It also conceals the end grain on head casings that are butted, rather than mitered, to the side casings.

Cap moldings are fitted over wainscot, head casing, basemolding and other trim pieces with visible edge grain to improve their appearance.

Chair, picture & shelf rail. Picture rail is installed around a room at the ceiling or between the ceiling and the tops of window and door head casings. These moldings feature a large curved bead along the top edge of the profile, which can be used to hold metal hooks for hanging pictures from wire (although, these days picture molding is used more often to reproduce a period look or simply as decoration). *Chair rail* is intended to protect wall surfaces from damage caused by collisions with chair backs. Some types of chair rail are outfitted with pegs so chairs can be hung from the walls when not in use or to get them up and out of the way for floor cleaning. Chair rail can now be found in most any room of the home, serving for the most part as a visual divider between the lower 3 ft. of wall surface and the wall above it. *Shelf rail* is hung on the wall either at eye level or near the ceiling, where it is used mostly to display plates and decorative objects (it's often called "plate rail" or "plate shelf" for this reason). Most shelf rail is created by joining several different molding types, from traditional to contemporary.

Chair, picture & shelf rail are attached to walls to fulfill the practical and decorative functions implied by their names.

Material options. Moldings are available in a variety of wood species. Your local building center or lumberyard likely will stock moldings in the most common hardwoods, like red oak, Phillipine mahogany, maple, birch and poplar, as well as softwoods like pine, hemlock, fir or cedar. The variety of wood types makes it possible to match trim to your doors, windows and cabinets, but this really only matters if your woodwork has a natural wood finish.

The molding industry divides moldings into two main categories: *stain grade* and *paint grade.* Stain-grade molding is milled from premium grade lumber and it is largely free of blemishes because it is intended to be clearcoated or stained. Most hardwood molding that you'll buy off the shelf is stain grade, and you'll pay more for it than softwood moldings like pine or fir. Hardwood varieties aren't always more expensive than softwood moldings, but generally this is the case. Paint-grade moldings, on the other hand, are primarily a mix of various pines and firs as well as poplar, because these woods have a consistent grain pattern that accepts paint well. Some manufacturers pre-prime the moldings at the factory so they're ready for paint right off the shelf. Softwood moldings can be stained too, of course, but differences in grain density can make the finish look splotchy.

Increasingly, moldings are being made out of synthetic materials. Depending upon the manufacturer,

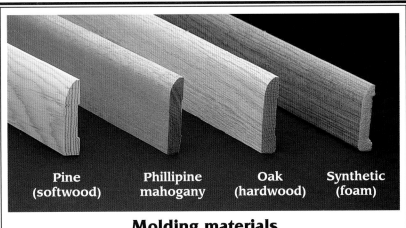

| Pine (softwood) | Phillipine mahogany | Oak (hardwood) | Synthetic (foam) |

Molding materials

Common wood types used for moldings include oak, Phillipine mahogany (lauan) and pine. Recently, manufacturers introduced paintable moldings made from reconstituted wood and other products. While inexpensive and suitable for some applications, synthetic moldings are not as durable as genuine wood products. TIP: When trying to match wood tones with the rest of the trim in your home, dab a little water on the molding sample. The wet color will be close to the actual color when a clear topcoat is applied.

synthetic moldings may be made of polyurethane foam, wood fiber-reinforced polyester or polystyrene. You'll also find trim made of medium-density fiberboard (MDF) or even vinyl-coated particleboard. Synthetic moldings are less expensive than solid wood moldings, and they can be manufactured in strips of just about any length. They're easy to distinguish from wood moldings because synthetics usually are primed in white or gray and have no distinctive wood grain on the back side. They're lightweight, and some varieties are extremely flexible. Some synthetic moldings are available with a faux wood grain paper bonded to the visible surfaces.

So, how do you choose between these materials? The most obvious factor to consider is *cost.* Stain-grade hardwood molding will cost more per foot than paint-grade trim and nearly twice as much as synthetics. If you are only installing one room's worth of trim, the extra expense may not be an issue. But if you're setting out to trim your entire house, the cost differences between hardwood, softwood or synthetic moldings could substantially impact your project budget. Regardless of which material type you choose for the molding, the more elaborate your trim scheme, the more you'll pay per foot. A three-piece baseboard, for instance, likely will cost twice as much as a single-piece baseboard.

Another factor to keep in mind is *workability.* Hardwood moldings are easy to cut and install with a power miter saw and a pneumatic nail gun, but they are much less forgiving than softwoods or synthetics if you plan to use a hand saw and hammer. Plan on drilling pilot holes for all of the nails and spending more time planing, sanding and filing to get the joints

MDF AS A MOLDING MATERIAL

MDF (medium-density fiberboard) is growing fast in popularity as a durable and inexpensive molding material that you can shape easily into just about any molding profile you want.

to fit tightly. Hardwood moldings are also more rigid than paint-grade moldings, and the wider the molding the more stiff they become. If your home has uneven walls, floors and ceilings, oak molding will create more gaps than synthetics or pine, which are easier to flex and conform to uneven surfaces. All in all, if you are an experienced woodworker or do-it-yourselfer and comfortable with tools, workability is less of a concern. But consider using softwoods or synthetics for your first few trim projects if you are just getting started.

Trim *durability* is a third issue to keep in mind when you are choosing molding. Stain-grade hardwoods will stand up best to nicks, dings and scratches because the wood is harder than either of the other options. But if you damage clearcoated hardwood molding, it will be more difficult to repair than simply puttying and repainting softwood trim. Synthetic molding is the least durable choice when it comes to resisting abrasion; it dents and crushes easily. It also won't hold nails as well as solid wood trim, so it's more likely to come loose unless you glue and nail it securely. One advantage to synthetic molding is that it is impervious to water, so it won't rot or discolor like wood if it gets wet (reconstituted wood products are an exception).

Aside from the material options, the larger issue of choosing moldings boils down to which specific style and effect you are trying to achieve. If you are simply trying to match new trim to existing trim in your home, your challenge will be to find moldings with identical or similar profiles, then finish them so they blend in with other trimwork. Don't be surprised if your local lumberyard or home center's selection of moldings doesn't match the molding profile you need, especially if you live in a home more than 50 years old. *TIP: You may be able to remove molding from inconspicuous areas of your home, like closets, and reuse it in more visible places for the sake of a good match. Install the newer moldings in closets instead, where the mismatch with the older moldings won't matter.*

For a wider selection of molding profiles, find a lumberyard in your area that does custom milling. They'll usually have a good selection of moldings on hand that may better suit your needs. Some will even grind knives for their milling machine to match the exact molding profile you're after or may have the knives on hand already from another job. Expect to pay a premium if you want custom-made moldings throughout your home.

Estimating material needs

If you are only trimming one door or window, it's easy to "ballpark" the amount of molding you'll need to wrap around the opening, and the amount of extra trim that's left on the shop floor probably won't matter much. If you're trimming all the doors, windows and walls in a new addition, however, it pays to be more prudent when estimating quantities of molding.

Trim carpenters group moldings into two categories: *standing trim* and *running trim*. Running trim "runs" horizontally around a room; baseboard and shoe, crown, chair rail and picture rail are the most common types. Standing trim refers to case moldings that wrap around windows, doors and room entryways. The real difference between these two groupings has to do with where joints are advisable. For windows and doors, strips of case molding should break and form joints only in the upper and lower corners, not along the sides or across the top. Standing moldings should be purchased long enough to fit around a door or window without having to make extra joints. On the other hand, running trim can be installed along a wall in random lengths, with the joints occurring wherever one piece ends and another begins.

You won't see moldings grouped in batches of "standing" or "running trim" at the lumberyard, however. In practice, moldings are used interchangeably between applications. You will notice, however, that moldings are sold by the linear foot in lengths starting at 7 or 8 ft. and increasing in 2-ft. increments up to 16 ft. They're sized this way because a standard door or window width is less than 4 ft., and interior doors are just under 7 ft. tall. Each 7-or 8-ft. strip of molding off the shelf can usually serve as a single side casing or two head casings. Longer lengths of molding can make combinations of side, head and sill casings with minimal waste.

Standing trim. Here's an example of how to measure standing trim. Imagine trimming the case moldings in a room with two interior doors. The trim width you plan to use is 2¼ in. The width of each door jamb from inside edge to inside edge is 32 in., and the doors have a standard jamb length of 80 in. In this case, you'd need one 7 or 8-ft. length of molding for each of the side casings. Calculate the actual side casing length by adding the jamb length (80 in.) plus 2¼ in. of molding for the miter joint at the top plus ¼ in. for the distance the molding is set back from the door frame, which totals 82½ in. Another 7 or 8-ft. strip would yield enough material for the two head casings. Each needs to be 32 in., plus 5½ in. for the pair of miters on each end, plus ½ in. for two ¼ in. setbacks, or 38 in. overall. To case the doors on one side then, you'd need a total of five 7 or 8-ft. strips of molding. Since most interior doors receive case molding on both sides of the door opening, multiply by two to estimate the total amount needed.

Running trim. Simply measure the perimeter of the room, including the openings for doors or entryways. The total equals the amount of lineal feet of molding you should buy. The overage caused by adding in the length of room openings serves as your "fudge factor."

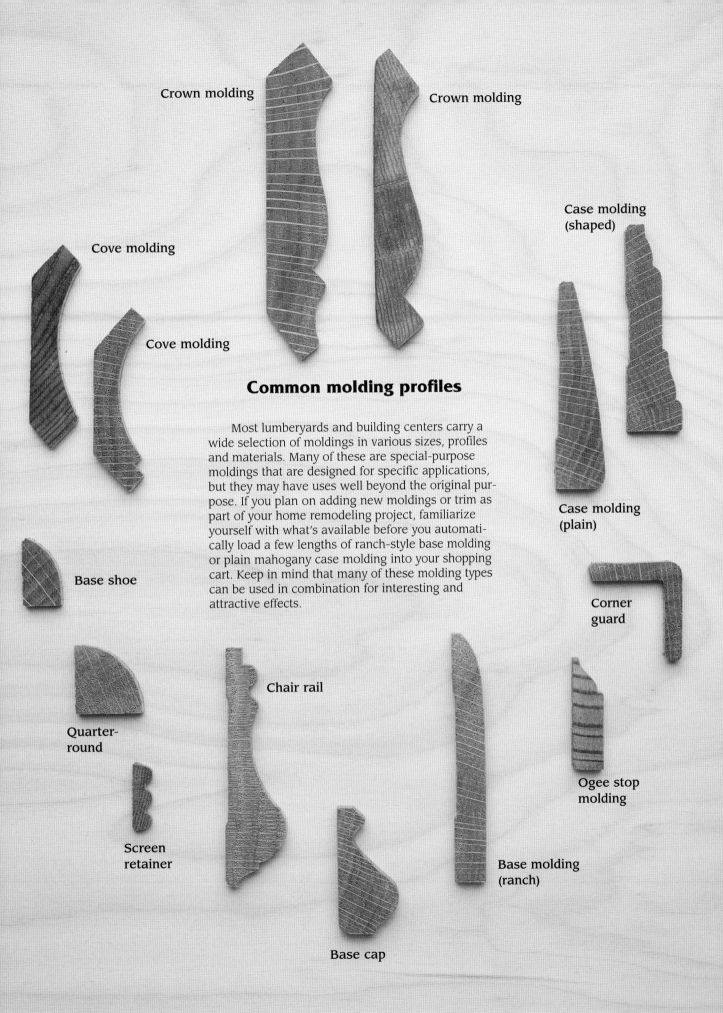

Crown molding

Crown molding

Case molding
(shaped)

Cove molding

Cove molding

Common molding profiles

Most lumberyards and building centers carry a wide selection of moldings in various sizes, profiles and materials. Many of these are special-purpose moldings that are designed for specific applications, but they may have uses well beyond the original purpose. If you plan on adding new moldings or trim as part of your home remodeling project, familiarize yourself with what's available before you automatically load a few lengths of ranch-style base molding or plain mahogany case molding into your shopping cart. Keep in mind that many of these molding types can be used in combination for interesting and attractive effects.

Case molding
(plain)

Corner
guard

Base shoe

Chair rail

Quarter-
round

Ogee stop
molding

Screen
retainer

Base molding
(ranch)

Base cap

Tools for Trim Carpentry

You don't need a truckload of tools to install trim accurately and efficiently, but to get professional-looking results you'll need more than a tape measure, hammer and circular saw. This section is intended to briefly review those tools that will make your trim projects go more smoothly and accurately. The tools are organized into small groups based on the functions they serve. You'll see that most of the tools on the following pages are fairly common, inexpensive carpentry tools. You probably own many or all of them already. Some of the more expensive tools, like power miter saws and air-compressor-driven pneumatic nail guns, are inexpensive to rent, which is a good option if your project budget won't allow a major tool purchase or if you don't have much trim to install.

Measuring & marking tools

In a nutshell, trim carpentry is about making tight-fitting joints. The absence of gaps or misfits between moldings is what sets a well-done trim project apart from one that looks like it was completed by an amateur. The trouble is, walls and ceilings are seldom flat and window and door frames may or may not be plumb, level or straight. So trim carpentry really is a task of trying to achieve uniformity and perfection to the eye while dealing with the many imperfect factors you'll find in a room. Measuring and marking moldings carefully and accurately is the first step toward installing trim successfully. Here are the tools you'll need for this stage of the task:

Tape measure. The length of the tape isn't as important in trim work as making sure your tape measure has an end hook that is solidly riveted to the tape. If the end hook slips in its mounting holes and you read the tape from the end, your measurements may vary by 1/16 in. or more, depending on whether you are pulling or pushing the tape to take a measurement. While this difference is negligible if you are rough-framing a wall, it makes all the difference for trim work, so buy a tape with a snug-fitting hook. Also, choose a tape with graduations that are easy for you to read, regardless of which side of the tape you are measuring from. For larger trimming projects, a 25-ft. tape should provide all the length you'll need for even the longest runs of wall in a room.

Squares. A *combination* or *try square* is essential for marking square ends on parts to be cut. Both tools are also handy to have on hand for adjusting power-miter-saw or table-saw blades for square. A combination square is particularly versatile, because it also measures 45° angles—the primary angle for making miter joints. Also, since the blade slides and locks, it can be set at a specific distance from the head of the tool for marking reveals on window and door casings. You may also want to add a *carpenter's (framing) square* to your tool box for checking window and door rough openings for square. It also doubles as a handy straightedge.

Bevel gauge. Not all miter joints form 90° corners. Non-square miter joints are common when hanging crown molding or wrapping baseboard around wall corners. In these instances, a bevel gauge can be set and locked to match any angle and used as a guide for marking trim parts. Get one with an adjustment knob

MEASURING TOOLS

Tape measure

Carpenter's (framing) square

Try square

Combination square

Sliding bevel gauge

Protractor

or lever that locks the blade solidly so the angle doesn't shift while you're marking parts. It's a good idea to carry a *protractor* with your bevel gauge for determining angles—the two tools go hand in hand. A protractor will measure angles up to 180°, and you can find them in the school supply section of most department stores.

Compass. In many instances it will be impossible to bend and fit a straight piece of molding to a floor or ceiling that is sagging or wavy. The way around this problem is to scribe a parallel mark along the molding that matches the contour of the surface it will butt against, then trim the molding to shape so it fits snug. The trim carpenter's preferred tool for this task is an ordinary *drafting compass* with a point on one leg and a sharp pencil outfitted in the other leg.

Other marking tools. Keep a sharp *pencil* and *carpenter's pencil* close at hand when you're marking trim. Aside from the usual purposes of these items, either one can serve as a scribing tool by laying the pencil flat against the surface being scribed and dragging it along the molding you are marking for the scribe. For more precise marking, reach for a sharp *scratch awl, pocket knife* or *utility knife.* Awls work best for marking wood across the grain, and pocket or utility knife blades are better suited for marking wood along the grain. You'll also find specialized marking knives with blades sharpened to a bevel on one edge only. The flat face of the blade is designed for marking against a

SCRIBING TOOLS

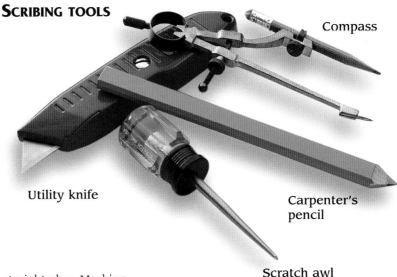

Compass

Utility knife

Carpenter's pencil

Scratch awl

straightedge. Marking knives work wonderfully, but unless you plan to install lots of trim, a marking knife probably isn't worth adding to your trim tool collection.

Levels and plumb bobs. It's important to check whatever you're trimming for plumb, square and level before you install the trim. If, for instance, a window frame or door jamb isn't plumb, square and level, you'll have to account for the deviations when you cut and fit the molding joints. Wainscot must be installed level to the floor, and it doesn't take much drift up or down from level to be noticeable, even at a casual glance. For general trimming, keep a *torpedo level* as well as a *2-ft. level* and a *4-ft. level* handy. You'll also want to add a *plumb bob* to your toolbox. Floors and ceilings are not reliable reference planes for checking other surfaces, like walls, for plumb. Instead, suspend a plumb bob from a point near the top of a wall and it will

provide an absolutely accurate measure of perpendicularity for checking the wall as well as door or window jambs.

Cutting tools

Trim is such a highly visible element when it wraps a window or door because we see the profiles, reveals and joinery close to eye level. For this reason, it's important to measure and cut trim accurately and cleanly, with no splintering or ragged edges. A clean cut is the product of a sharp blade and a saw that you can control precisely during the cut. In trim work, you'll discover that often it will take several cuts following the first cut to make moldings fit together the way you need them to. The more control you have over where the blade meets the cutting line, the more you'll be able to use the saw like a hand plane for making precision trim cuts. Here are the best saws for the job:

Power miter saw or table saw. Professional-quality power miter saws are commonplace these days among weekenders, as well as the pros. A power miter saw is the

LEVELS

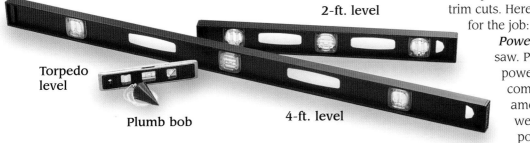

2-ft. level

Torpedo level

Plumb bob

4-ft. level

right choice for cutting trim. Basically, the tool amounts to a circular saw mounted on an arm that pivots down over an adjustable saw base. The base swivels right or left and can be locked to any angle up to 45°, or even slightly more on some models. These tools make precise, clean cuts in both hardwoods and softwoods, especially when outfitted with the proper blade. For occasional trim work, buy or rent a saw with an 8- or 10-in.-dia. blade. A *Compound miter saw,* so named because the blade angle can be adjusted both vertically and horizontally, is useful if you need to cut crown molding wider than about 5 in. For general-purpose trim work, however, the compound angle-cutting feature of these miter saws is unnecessary—even if you are cutting crown molding. For cleanest cuts, outfit the saw with a 60 to 100-tooth carbide-tipped blade.

If you'd rather not invest in a power miter saw, a *table saw* or *radial arm saw* will also do a good job of cutting molding accurately, but neither of these saws are as

HAND SAWS

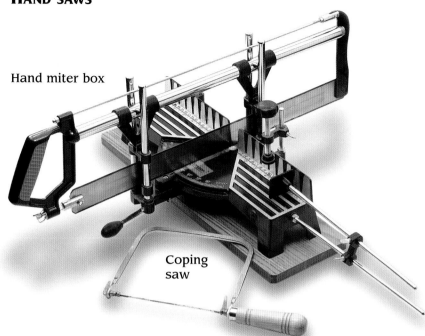

Hand miter box

Coping saw

well-suited for trim work as a power miter saw. When cutting moldings on a table saw, set the miter gauge carefully and hold the workpiece tightly against the miter gauge. If the molding moves even the slightest bit laterally during a miter cut, it will ruin the accuracy

of the cut. Check your miter gauge settings by cutting a piece of scrap molding before committing to the final cut on your workpiece.

Hand saws. An inexpensive and invaluable hand saw for shaping molding is the *coping saw.* The frame of the saw is shaped like a

POWER MITER SAWS

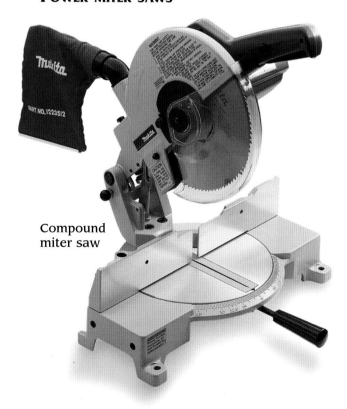

Compound miter saw

Sliding compound miter saw

"C", and it holds an extremely narrow, fine-toothed blade under tension for cutting intricate curves. Coping saws get their name because they're designed to make cope cuts (cuts that follow the profile of a molding so it can fit tightly against the profile of another molding).

If you prefer to cut joints manually with a hand saw and traditional miter box, use a sharp, fine-toothed backsaw (the back of the saw blade is stiffened with a metal spine) or the miter box saw that comes with the miter box.

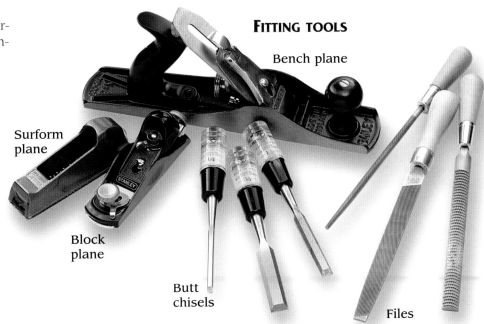

Bench plane

Surform plane

Block plane

Butt chisels

Files

Fitting tools

Once you've marked and cut strips of molding to length and shaped the ends into angles for joints, the remainder of the trimming task boils down to fitting the pieces against one another until the joints close without force or gaps. Careful and sometimes tedious fitting and refitting involves a good dose of patience and a few more tools in the arsenal:

Block plane and chisels. For trimming away the waste of shallow scribes, as well as shaving miter and butt joints, few tools do the job as well as a sharp block plane. An even better choice for trim work is a *low-angle block plane,* so named because the blade of the plane forms a shallower angle to the wood than an ordinary block plane. The lower blade angle allows the plane to shave end grain without splintering or crushing it in the process. You may also want to keep a *bench plane* handy for shaping longer molding edges, but a belt or disk sander can also do the job. Sharp *butt chisels* (the type with metal caps on the ends of the handles) are indispensable for cutting hinge mortises and paring away extra material, such as when you're trimming back-bevels onto the ends of baseboard.

Files and rasps. The best tool for cleaning up an intricate cope cut is a *file.* For filing small contours, invest in a *rattail file,* which has a cylindrical rod with cutting teeth formed all around the rod. As far as other files are concerned, have at least one file with a partially-rounded profile and a flat face in both coarse and fine cutting grades for general contour work. Keep a rasp or two in your toolbox for more aggressive stock removal as well as a *Surform plane* (a plane-style body with a coarse, tempered rasp for a sole plate), which is handy for shaving down wallboard paper and built-up wallboard compound.

Fastening tools

There's probably no nailing task more delicate than attaching trim molding. The moldings themselves are thin and easy to split. You'll find your-

self driving nails a fraction of an inch from the floor or ceiling and often holding an unwieldy length of floppy molding in the process. It's critical that moldings are held securely while you drive the nails so the joints don't open up. If all of this isn't enough to keep in mind, all it takes is one errant hammer blow to smash a delicate molding profile that will be difficult to repair. Choose your fastening tools carefully.

Hammer and nailsets. If you plan to install molding with a hammer and nails, select a hammer that is a comfortable weight for you and has a smooth face on the hammerhead. If the face of the hammerhead has a checkered pattern, it is intended for framing tasks, not trim work. Hammer weights vary between 16 and 20 ounces, so swing a few and choose

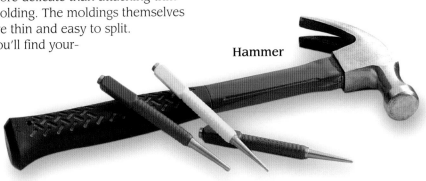

Hammer

Nailsets (3 sizes)

the one that you can handle comfortably and accurately above your head, as well as next to the floor.

Buy and use a set of *nailsets* to drive the nailheads the final ¼ in. or so into the trim, rather than using the hammerhead directly. Finish nails have extremely small heads that are easy to miss if you are nailing at an awkward angle or you are fatigued. Nailsets will keep the hammerhead a safe distance away from the molding, but their actual purpose is to allow the nailhead to be driven slightly below the surface of the wood without marring it. Nailsets look like metal punches and have concave tips that fit around the nailhead to keep the nailset from slipping off the nail as you drive it home. They come in several sizes. The better sets are coded by color so you can determine the size of the tip at a glance.

Pneumatic nail guns. A faster and more foolproof way to install trim is to use an air-powered nailgun. Nailguns are designed to drive a nail into the wood and beneath the surface in one action. With a nailgun, there's no weight to swing; simply hold the gun in place against the trim and squeeze the trigger to drive

PNEUMATIC NAILERS

Brad nailer

Finish nailer

the nail. Even better, it takes only one hand to operate a nailgun, which leaves your other hand free to position the trim and hold it steady while you fasten it. The same task is next to impossible to do with a hammer. Nailguns are somewhat expensive to buy but cheap to rent, and the nails are available at any home center. A *finish nailer,* a *brad nailer* and a *crown stapler* all have multiple applications in trim carpentry.

Trim removal tools

Undoubtedly, you'll need to remove a piece of trim from time to time, despite your best efforts to install every piece perfectly. Or, you may want to remove sections of existing trim without damaging them so they can be reused. A good tool for pulling trim away from other surfaces is a *paint scraper* or a *putty knife* with a flat, spring-steel blade. These semi-flexible blades are thin enough to slip between moldings and walls without damaging either surface, yet stout enough so you can use the tool as a lever to work the molding loose. Once you've opened a gap of sufficient size, switch to a small prybar to complete the task. Another good trick for removing trim is to use plain old wood shims—simply drive them behind the trim piece. This works especially well for removing case molding.

TRIM REMOVAL TOOLS

Putty knife

Flat prybar

Wood shims

Fasteners & adhesives

It's a good idea to be aware of your options for fastening trim. They include nails (regular and pneumatic), screws and adhesive (glue and construction adhesive).

Finish (casing) nails. Almost without exception, you'll use conventional or pneumatic finish nails to install trim. Finish nails are designed with small, compact nailheads that are easy to conceal with wood putty. The thin nail shanks penetrate wood fibers easily to keep the trim from splitting. Conventional finish nails are sized using the pennyweight system, which is designated by a number next to a "d" (which stands for penny). The higher the number, the longer the nail and, eventually, the thicker the shank. Manufacturers often list the nail length on the box as well. A good range of finish nails to keep on hand is from 3d (1¼ in. long) to 8d (2½ in.). Pneumatic nails are sold by nail length and wire gauge thickness. Choose 16-or18-gauge (ga.) nails for driving through delicate or thinner trim and 15-gauge nails for wider or thicker trim and hardwood. Select the same fastener length for pneumatic nails as you would for conventional finish nails.

Screws. In cases where you are installing trim over a wall surface that deflects easily, lacks sufficient nailing surface, or is framed with metal studs, use screws instead of nails to attach moldings. Two screw types that are suitable for trimwork are common *wallboard screws* and less-common *trimhead screws.* Trimhead screws look like wallboard screws, but the threads aren't as coarse and the heads are much smaller, so they're easier to conceal. Both type of screws are self-tapping, which means they bore their own pilot hole to minimize splitting, and the threads are hardened to bite into metal wall studs. Trimhead screws are square-drive and wallboard screws are available with several head configurations. Phillips or square-drive work well for trim work. Whether you use wallboard or trimhead screws, the downside to screws in general is that you'll spend more time patching over the screwheads than you will with nails. As much as possible, try to reserve screws for trimwork that will have a painted finish.

ADHESIVES

Yellow wood glue (carpenter's glue)

Construction adhesive

Adhesives. Keep a tube of multipurpose *construction adhesive* around for trim projects. A dab behind a piece of trim may hold it tight in an area where there is no wall framing to secure it with nails. Use *yellow wood glue* or even white glue to cover the mating ends of butt and miter joint parts. The glue will provide some degree of bonding strength but also will seal the wood pores from absorbing moisture, swelling and opening the glue joint.

FINISH NAILS (ACTUAL SIZE)

16d casing

10d casing

8d finish

6d finish

4d finish

3d finish

SCREWS (ACTUAL SIZE)

Trimhead screw

Wallboard screw

PNEUMATIC NAILS (ACTUAL SIZE)

18 ga.

15 ga.

Making Your Own Molding

A good option to buying moldings off the shelf or having them custom-made at a millwork shop is to cut your own in your own shop. In addition to saving quite a bit of money, routing your own moldings may be a sensible alternative for your project if you can't find premilled molding in the profile you like, or if it isn't available in the same wood species as the rest of your woodwork. To make moldings, you'll need a router mounted in a router table and and an assortment of bits (or, alternatively, a table saw outfitted with a molding head cutter). A third tool that's ideal for making moldings is a stationary shaper, which operates on the same principle as a router in a router table, except a shaper has a much larger motor and a thicker spindle. Shapers are designed to spin large, three-bladed cutters that look like giant router bits. Cabinet shops use them all the time for manufacturing raised panels and door frame joints, but shapers aren't common home shop tools because they are expensive.

A router is a safer and less expensive tool for making molding than a table saw and molding head cutter. Router bits take much smaller bites of wood, so the cuts are safer to make. Plus, router bits come in scores of different profiles to mill all or part of virtually any molding profile you can imagine. When the tool is used correctly, the profiles produced by a router are as smooth as those made with a shaper. As far as cost is concerned, top-quality routers are readily available and relatively inexpensive. It's worth spending a little extra to buy a router that can be run at variable speeds so you can run it more slowly when using larger bits. Also, invest in a router that will accept ½-in.-dia.-shank bits. Bits with ½-in. shanks are more expensive

but they will hold up to more stress and heat than the smaller ¼-in. shank bits.

The best set-up for cutting molding with a router is to mount a router of at least 1½ HP in a router table equipped with an adjustable fence. This way, you'll be able to focus your attention on feeding the wood into the bit without also having to manipulate the router over the wood. You can also mill much narrower stock on a router table.

A router table is a simple accessory consisting of a small tabletop with a router hanging inverted beneath it so the router bit can be raised and lowered through the table. Router tables have an adjustable fence that can be positioned closer to or further from the bit, depending on the cutting operation and the width of the wood being cut. The height of the bit, which will affect the shape that it cuts, can be raised or lowered. You can buy a router table from most home centers or woodworking supply catalogs, but many woodworkers prefer to build their own.

The process for cutting molding with a router table involves passing a strip of wood on-edge or on its face against the fence and past the spinning router bit to cut a profile. The settings you use for bit height and the distance from the fence to the bit depend on a number of factors: where the profile needs to be in relation to the edge of the board, how much wood you need to remove to make the shape, and the style of the cutter itself. For instance, a basemolding that has an ogee profile along the top edge and a pair of flutes near the bottom will require several bit and fence changes as well as three or more passes of the workpiece over the tool: at least one bit and fence setting to cut the ogee, a bit and fence change for cutting one flute, then a final fence position change for cutting the second flute. If you're cutting hardwood, it's a good idea to rout a profile in several passes, raising the bit each time in ⅛ to ¼-in. increments to prevent the router from bogging down or making very ragged cuts.

Regardless of the kind of molding you're routing, start with clear, flat, straight boards. For best results, it's a good idea to run the edges of your workpieces over a jointer first to flatten them all along their length. Bowed or cupped edges will result in inconsistent routing. If you don't own a jointer, flatten the board edges by ripping them on a table saw with the rip fence aligned parallel with the blade.

Spend some time before you begin routing and think about the safest way to organize your cuts and router set-up. It's important to orchestrate the cutting so workpieces won't wobble or tip on the router table after the first pass. Rout the smallest details of the profile first, if possible, and save the larger curves or cut-out areas for last. For milling moldings narrower than about 1½ in., the safest approach is to rout them on stock that's at least 4 to 6 in. wide, then rip-cut the

A router table in an invaluable router accessory for cutting your own moldings. Equip it with a variable-speed router that's at least 1½ HP, preferably with a "soft start" power-up feature.

(Continued page 24)

Router bits

It doesn't take dozens of bits to cut moldings. A good starter set consists of the following:

- Straight bits (½, ⅜, ¼ in.) for cutting rabbets, flat-bottomed grooves and reveals
- Corebox bit for cutting round-bottomed grooves (called flutes)
- Cove, roundover and Roman ogee bits for cutting concave and convex curves
- Chamfer bit for milling angled edges
- V-groove bit for cutting tapered grooves (called veining)

Combination router bits are also available. They can cut more than one kind of profile, depending on how far the bit is raised above the table and how much it extends out from the router table fence. At one bit height, the exposed portion of the cutter might create an ogee curve, and raising the bit a little higher will add a thin reveal or maybe a roundover to the profile (See page 27).

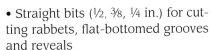

Roman ogee bit

Round over bit

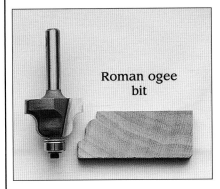

Straight bit

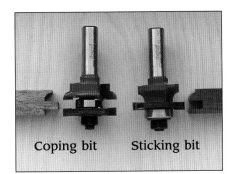

Coping bit   Sticking bit

Chamfering bit

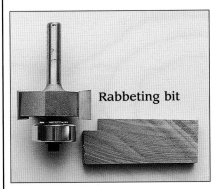

Rabbeting bit

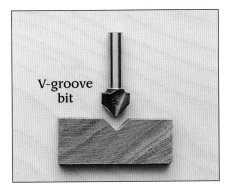

V-groove bit

Core-box bit

Panel bit

Cove bit

(Continued from page 22)

molding free from the wider workpiece on a table saw. Rout both long edges of the board rather than just one, then cut each edge free to double your productivity. For milling short lengths of molding, always start with a workpiece that's long enough (at least 10 in.) to hold safely on the router table. Once you've cut the profile,

cross-cut the molding to its required length. Never have more of the router bit exposed than is needed to make the cut.

The sequence of cuts you'll need to make to rout different moldings will vary with each type of molding you make. A few examples, and the steps required to make them, are shown in the next few pages.

TIP: INSTALL A SACRIFICIAL FENCE

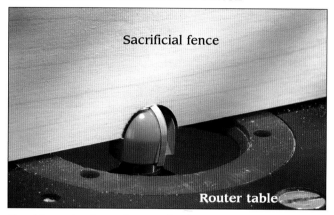

Bits without a bearing, such as core box bits, can be shielded by attaching a length of flat scrap against the router fence to serve as a sacrificial fence. With the bit installed, turn on the router and raise the bit slowly into the sacrificial fence to the height you need. This way, the fence forms a tight guard around the bit. A sacrificial fence is particularly useful with combination router bits to expose just the amount of profile needed for making a particular cut.

USING PILOTED BITS IN A ROUTER TABLE

When making edge cuts with bits that have a built-in pilot bearing, set the fence so it covers all but the leading edge of the bearing and, in turn, half the diameter of the cutter.

HOW TO MAKE SINGLE-PROFILE MOLDING

1 Set up your router table with the bit you'll use (all edge-cutting router bits can be used to make moldings—a cove bit is being used above to make cove molding). Make test cuts, adjusting the bit height and fence position until you find the best set-up for the molding you want. Run both edges of a piece of wide stock through the bit.

2 Rip-cut the moldings to desired width on your table saw. Cut one edge free, then reset the fence to cut off the other edge as well. Always use a featherboard and hold-down as you guide the workpiece through the saw blade.

Making base cap

You can mill your own base cap molding using a router table with an ogee bit and a beading bit. You'll also need your table saw to rabbet the backs of the molding strips and to rip them to width. Base cap is used most often on top of basemolding, but you can also use it to cap wainscot or, by eliminating the back rabbet, you can use if as chair rail.

1 Set up your router table with a classic ogee or ogee bit and mill an ogee profile in both edges of a board that's at least 6 in. wide.

2 Replace the ogee bit with a beading bit and adjust the cutting height so the beading bit cuts a bead in the workpiece at the top of the ogee (you'll want to have plenty of scrap for testing your set-up before cutting the actual workpieces).

3 Use your table saw to cut the rabbets in the back of the workpiece (a dado-blade set will save a lot of time). The rabbets should be sized to fit whatever size board you're capping (minus any rabbets on the board—See next step).

4 Cut a matching rabbet groove in the top, front edge of the basemolding (or whatever board you're capping), using your table saw and a dad-blade set, if you have one.

5 Rip-cut the base cap pieces from the workpieces. The cut should be made exactly at the top edge of the rabbet cut in the back of the workpiece. Always cut the workpiece so the molding strip is not pinned between the blade and the fence.

1 Fluted moldings can be used in just about any trim carpentry application to dress up the look of the moldings. Most often, fluting is done on standing moldings, like door casing. The fluting is accomplished with a ½ in. core-box bit and a router. If you're not using a router table, you'll need to set up a jig to keep the cuts straight and parallel. The jig shown here simply consists of pairs of parallel strips of straight plywood that sandwich the workpiece and provide a guide for the router base. A wide spacer is tacked to the inside edge of one guide so the router base contacts both guides. The first outer flute is cut, then the workpiece is flipped and the opposite outer flute is cut.

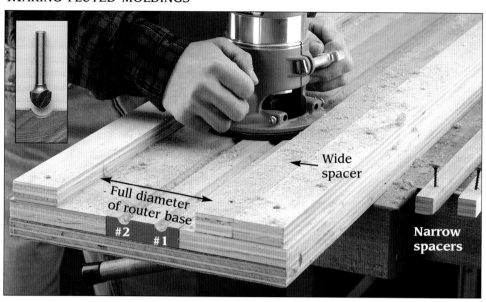

2 We replaced the wide spacer with a pair of narrower spacers, one tacked at the inside edge of each guide. The two narrower spacers center the router bit on the workpiece, while maintaining contact for guidance from both sides. This contact is important to keep the router from bouncing in the jig. Then, the center flute is cut. Even though the MDF stock shown here is relatively easy to work, we made each cut in two passes, increasing the cutting depth after the first pass.

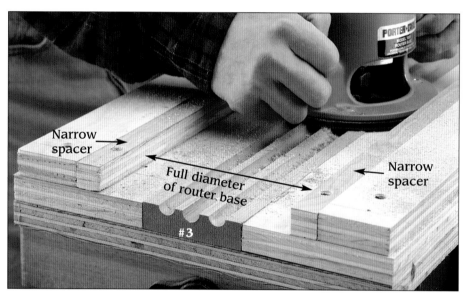

OPTION: Stopped flutes. For a truly elegant appearance, cut case moldings with rows of stopped fluting. The jig shown here is similar to the one used in steps 1 and 2 above, but it contains fixed router stops that span the cutting area. Also like the jig above, this one uses spacers to establish the cutting line for the router. But unlike the jig above, this one does not "trap" the router base, so you need to be a little more careful to maintain steady pressure against the guides and spacers as you cut.

Combination bits. If you need to make a sizable quantity of profiled molding, a combination bit with multiple profile-cutting options can save time and money. Combination router bits are capable of milling more than one profile, depending on which part on the cutting edge meets the workpiece. The bit shown above is positioned high enough to cut a double ogee (left photo). Were the bit lowered, it could be used to cut just a single ogee. By raising the bit in the router table, a bead-cutting profile is exposed (right photo).

Make-it-yourself molding ideas

Corner blocks: Decorative corner blocks (usually installed at the head joints in casing—see page 70) are surprisingly expensive when purchased at a millwork retailer. One solution is to make your own with top-bearing profile cutters deigned to be chucked into your drill press.

Plinth blocks: A three-sided guide jig can be used to guide profiled router cuts production-style. The jig above is being used to create a set of matching plinth blocks. You simply cut the stock to uniform size, then mill each piece, flipping the pieces to cut all edges.

Making moldings with a table saw

In addition to ripping strips of profiled stock, you can also use table saws for cutting profiles. There are two ways to go about it. One is to replace the saw blade with a molding head cutter that works very much like a shaper. The other is to feed the workpiece across the blade at an angle, cutting partially through the workpiece to create a cove. Both tasks are dangerous, so be sure to take all possible safety precautions (See your table saw owner's manual).

USING A MOLDING HEAD CUTTER

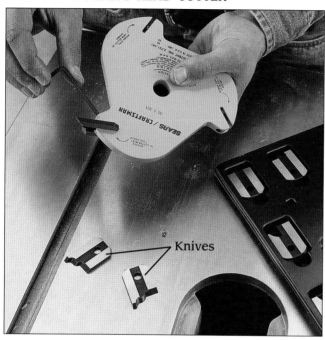

Molding heads consist of a heavy center hub with two to four slots for holding a set of profiled steel molding knives. Knives are available in a host of different shapes for cutting custom molding. Molding heads should only be used in a full-size saw with at least a 1½ HP motor.

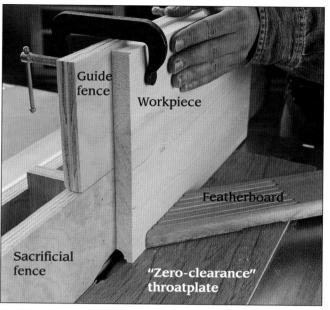

Setting up for the cut. Outfit your table saw with a sacrificial fence over the cutter and a "zero-clearance" throatplate made from thin plywood to keep the workpiece from dipping into the saw throat. For safety, clamp a guide fence to the top of the workpiece. The guide fence should ride smoothly on the top of the sacrificial fence. Always use a featherboard to guide the workpiece.

OPTION: Molding "tunnel." In cases where you must cut molding on narrow workpieces, create a "tunnel" from scrapwood to support and guide workpieces as you feed them over the knives (See illustration, right). Pushsticks alone will not give you the holding power you'll need to control your work. Use a scrap pushstick of the same dimensions as your workpieces to push the wood strips through the tunnel.

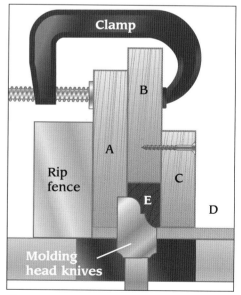

The molding "tunnel" consists of a sacrificial rip fence (A), a top support (B), side support (C) and either a zero-clearance throatplate or a piece of scrap plywood (D). The tunnel holds a workpiece (E) in place over the knives.

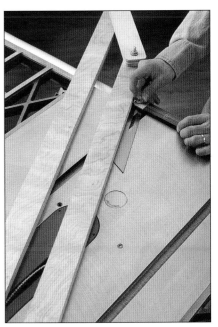

1 Draw a curved layout line on the end of your workpiece to mark the cove profile. Raise the blade above the saw table so the teeth at the top of the blade match the highest point of the cove profile.

2 Adjust the cove parallelogram jig so that the inside edges of the jig match the width of the cove profile. Set the jig on the saw table and over the blade. Turn the whole jig left or right until the inside edges of the jig touch the front and back edges of the blade (See inset photo). In this position, the jig sets the angle you'll need for cutting the cove.

3 Set a bevel gauge to match the angle the parallelogram jig forms with the front edge of the saw table. Be careful not to bump the parallelogram jig out of alignment as you set the angle on the tool.

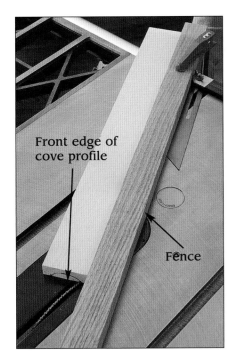

Front edge of cove profile

Fence

Fence

4 Select a length of flat stock about 4 ft. long to serve as a fence for guiding the workpiece when you cut the cove. Set the workpiece and fence on the saw table and against the bevel gauge. Shift the fence until the front blade teeth and the front edge of the cove profile intersect. Clamp the fence in place.

5 Using the workpiece as a spacer, clamp a second fence to the saw table, parallel to the first fence, to create a track for cutting the workpiece. Then cut the cove in a series of shallow passes, increasing the blade height about 1/16 in. with each pass.

Milling a partial cove. If your cove profile only needs to be a partial curve shape, cut a saw kerf into the fence you clamp to the saw table so the blade is partially buried in the fence. Cut the partial cove profile as you would a full cove, in shallow 1/16-in. passes.

Windows
& Doors

Windows & Doors

Trim for windows and doors consists mostly of case molding that is used to conceal the gaps between the jambs and the rough opening framing members. It also includes stools and aprons (the interior window sill). Even though there isn't a lot of range in the general types of trimming you'll need to do around doors and windows, you will find quite a number of choices for molding styles and the overall trimming schemes.

In this section you'll find clear descriptions of how to install the most popular door and window trim pieces. You'll also find a little bonus: since the most common time for trimming a door or window is after replacement of the old unit, we've included a refresher course on how to install doors and windows.

If you are hanging trim for the first time, doors and windows are a good place to start, because the procedure isn't all that difficult and you'll learn a variety of basic trim carpentry techniques that will help you with other trim projects.

CROSS-SECTION OF A WINDOW (DOUBLE-HUNG)

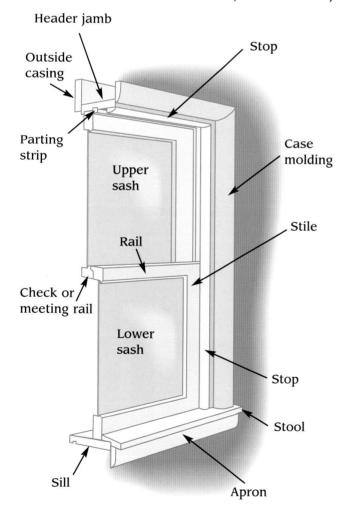

Header jamb

Outside casing

Parting strip

Stop

Upper sash

Rail

Case molding

Stile

Check or meeting rail

Lower sash

Stop

Stool

Sill

Apron

Nail window and door molding at the jambs and the framing members that form the rough opening. Keep in mind that there is almost always a gap between the jambs and framing members.

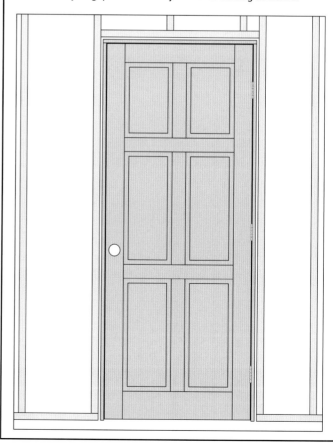

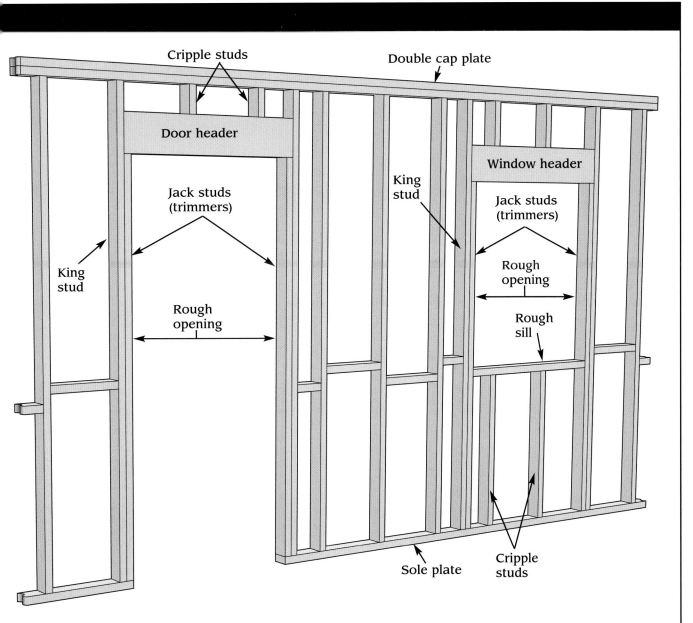

Cripple studs

Double cap plate

Door header

Jack studs
(trimmers)

King
stud

Window header

King
stud

Jack studs
(trimmers)

Rough
opening

King
stud

Rough
opening

Rough
sill

Sole plate

Cripple
studs

Window & door framing

If you've never built a wall or installed a window or door before, study the wall anatomy illustrations on these pages to familiarize yourself with how windows and doors are framed in a wall. Window and door locations in rough framing are called rough openings, and they are sized larger than the outside dimensions of the door and window jambs by about ½ to 1 in. The larger opening size allows the jambs to be installed and adjusted after the framing is complete. Door and window jambs are wedged into the rough openings with pairs of tapered shims that allow the jambs to be adjusted as needed until they are plumb, square and level in the wall framing.

Notice that window and door rough openings are reinforced on the sides and top with various kinds of

framing including headers, king studs and jack studs (also called trimmers). From a structural standpoint, this extra framing helps transfer the load of what's above the window or door safely around it and down to the bottom of the wall. As far as trim carpentry is concerned, this extra framing provides wider nailing surfaces for fastening the moldings in place. Generally, there's about 3 in. of solid framing on each side of a window or door jamb and at least 3½ in. above the top jamb piece, called the head jamb. Usually headers are even wider. Most windows have wider headers than interior doors, unless the doors are located in load-bearing walls. Rough sills, located below the bottom window jamb piece, may be either a single thickness of 2× lumber (1½ in.) or doubled up to 3 in. thickness, depending on how the wall was framed.

1 Pry off the case molding around the window with a flat prybar. Work carefully to avoid damaging the surrounding wall surfaces.

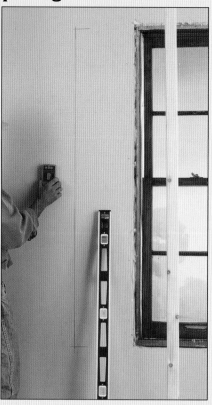

2 Locate the nearest wall stud outside the rough opening area, and draw a cutting line on the wallboard. The line should be centered over the wall stud to provide nailing surfaces for the new wallboard.

3 Remove the old window unit. To simplify the process, remove the sashes from the frame first. Free the frame by cutting nails that attach the frame to the wall studs with a reciprocating saw.

4 Use a level as a straightedge for marking cutting lines on the wall studs in the project area. Allow space for the new sill and header when laying out the cuts.

5 After installing temporary support, cut the wall studs to create the rough opening. Remove enough of each stud to allow for the sill and header. Avoid damage to the sheathing as you remove the studs.

Jack stud

<7/>Construct a header: We sandwiched a strip of ⅜-in. plywood between two pieces of 2-in. dimension lumber, then bonded the header with construction adhesive and 10d nails.

<8/>Set the header in position at the top of the window opening, and attach it by driving 10d nails through the king studs and into the ends of the header.

<6/>Nail a jack stud to each king stud on either side of the rough opening, using 10d nails spaced every 12 in. Jack studs extend from the wall's sole plate to the bottom of the planned header location.

<9/>Attach the double rough sill in two pieces. Cut two 2 × 4s to fit the width of the rough opening, then nail one of the 2 × 4s to the tops of the cripple studs. Face-nail the second 2 × 4 to the first one.

<10/>Drill holes through the exterior sheathing and siding at the four corners of the rough opening and connect the four holes with a straightedge. Cut the siding and sheathing along the reference lines with a circular saw or reciprocating saw. Continued next page

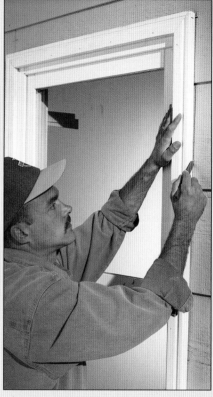

11 Remove siding and sheathing in the new rough opening area by cutting with a circular saw, then finishing the cuts with a chisel.

12 Set the new window into the opening, then shim it from inside until it's level and plumb in the opening.

13 Trace the outline of the brick mold onto the siding to scribe a cutting line, then remove the window from the opening.

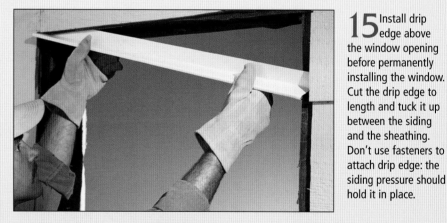

15 Install drip edge above the window opening before permanently installing the window. Cut the drip edge to length and tuck it up between the siding and the sheathing. Don't use fasteners to attach drip edge: the siding pressure should hold it in place.

16 Attach windows with preattached brick mold by driving 10d galvanized casing nails through the brick mold and sheathing and into the wall framing members. Drive the nailheads just below the surface with a nailset.

14 Wrap the surfaces of the framing members in the rough opening with building paper. Tuck the edges of the strips behind the sheathing, and staple.

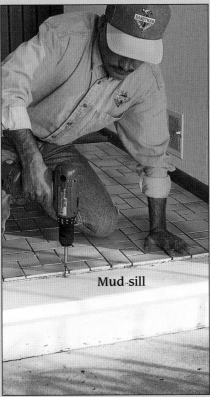

1 Remove the old door jamb assembly. Then clean up the rough opening by removing any old shims or nails that might interfere with the new installation.

2 Inspect the sill and replace it if needed. The sill shown above was in good condition, but we recoated it with primer/sealant since we had the chance. Drive a few deck screws to cinch the sill in place.

3 Apply caulk or panel adhesive to the back sides of the brickmold and to the top of the sill, then set the new door unit into the rough opening.

6 Adjust the threshold height so the bottom of the door just brushes the threshold when it closes. The threshold shown above has built-in height adjustment screws.

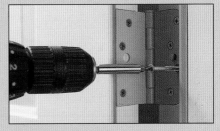

4 Shim between the jambs and the jack studs until the door is square in the opening, then secure the door with casing nails driven through shim locations.

5 Attach the brickmold to the wall studs with 10d galvanized casing nails. Make sure to keep the nails centered side to side so the brickmold doesn't split.

7 Replace one or two of the short hinge screws provided by the door manufacturer with 3-in. wood screws. The longer screws will penetrate all the way through the jamb and into the jack stud.

1 Use a flat prybar to remove the case molding on both sides of the doorway. The prybar should be applied on the jamb side of the doorway to avoid damaging the walls. Use care when prying the mitered corners; they're often lock-nailed through the miter from the top.

2 Use a reciprocating saw fitted with a metal-cutting remodeler's blade to cut through the casing nails that secure the jambs and header to the wall framing members. Once all the nails are cut, pull the old jamb out of the opening.

TIP: Prehung doors typically come with a spacer board attached to the bottoms of the side jambs. This temporary spacer must be removed before installing the door. An easy way to keep the jamb frame square when hanging the door is to nail a piece of scrap across the jamb opening before removing the bottom spacer. Cut the brace so that it overlaps but does not extend beyond the outside faces of the jambs. Once the door is shimmed and nailed into place, remove the brace.

3 With a few shims slipped into the gaps between the door jambs and the wall framing members, check the door unit to make sure it's level and plumb. Adjust as necessary. Also make sure preattached case molding is flush against the wall surface.

4 Insert pairs of shims between the hinge-side jamb and the rough opening. Position them behind each hinge and adjust them in or out until the hinge-side jamb is plumb.

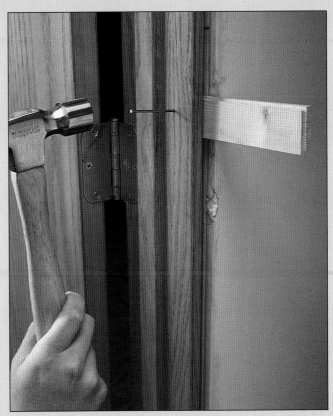

5 Nail the jamb in place with 8d casing (finish) nails, driving them through the shims and into the jack studs at the edge of the rough opening. Then close the door and shim the lock-side jamb until a 1/8-in. gap remains between the door and lock-side jamb. Nail the lock-side jamb through the shims as well.

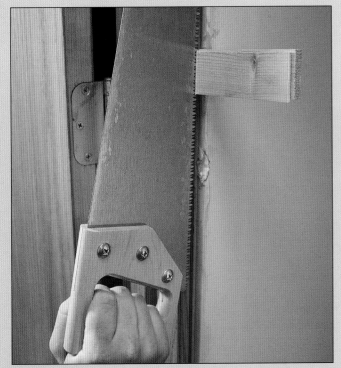

6 Use a hand saw to cut off the shims so they're flush with the edges of the door jambs. Hold the saw vertically when cutting to keep it from damaging the walls.

7 Install the door lockset assembly. The lock and bolt holes are pre-bored on prehung interior doors. Insert the latch bolt into the bolt hole so that the bevel side of the bolt faces the jamb. Then line up each half of the knob assembly with the bolt mechanism, and fit the knob assembly together. Secure the door lock assembly with the screws provided, according to the manufacturer's instructions.

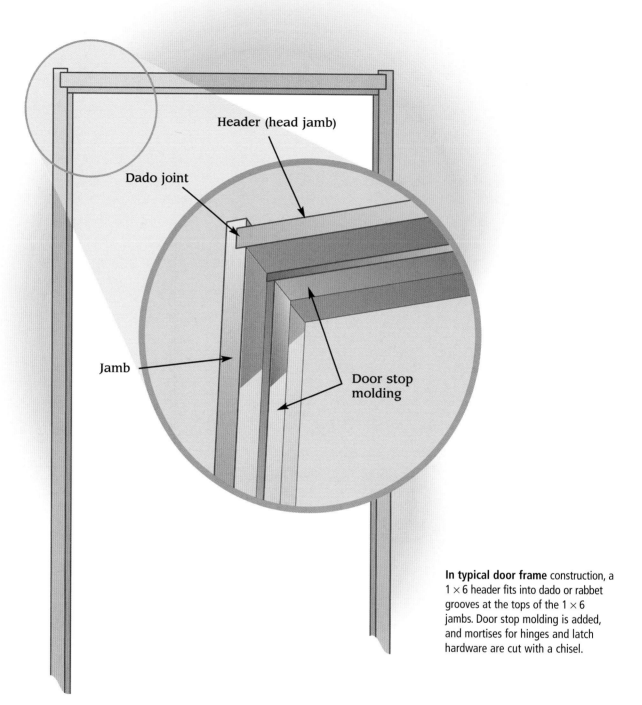

Header (head jamb)

Dado joint

Jamb

Door stop molding

In typical door frame construction, a 1 × 6 header fits into dado or rabbet grooves at the tops of the 1 × 6 jambs. Door stop molding is added, and mortises for hinges and latch hardware are cut with a chisel.

Building & installing custom door frames

While prehung doors are easy and convenient to install, they won't work in every home remodeling situation. Your existing door may be in fine shape, but the jamb and moldings are damaged or outdated; you might find the perfect door for your room at a salvage yard or even tucked away in a corner of your basement; or you may

decide to build your own custom door to fit a non-standard opening or to match a specific design you have in mind. In any of these situations, you'll need to create your own door frame from scratch, then hang and balance the door in the new frame.

Before starting, remove the old door and frame and measure the

rough opening for the door. Subtract ½ in. from each dimension to get the correct outside dimensions for the new frame. If you're planning to use dado joints to join the header to the jambs, be sure to add back an inch into the height of each jamb.

1 Cut the jambs and header to length from clear, straight 1 × 6 lumber. Remember to allow for the depth of the dadoes (3/8 in.) at the tops of the jambs when determining the size for the header. Cut 3/4-in.-wide × 3/8-in.-deep dadoes in the jambs at the header height. Make the cuts in two or three passes of increasing depth, using a router and 3/4-in. straight bit. If the rough opening has a rough header in the wall framing, you'll need to use rabbet joints at the tops of the jambs, not dadoes. For speed and consistency, gang-cut the jambs.

Straight bit

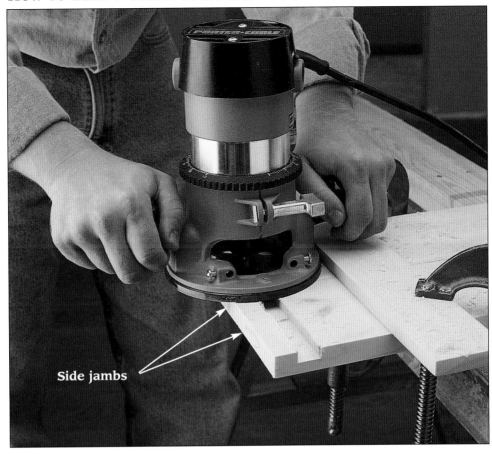

Side jambs

2 Glue the header into the dadoes in the jambs, and reinforce the joint with wood screws driven through the jambs and into the ends of the header. Lay the assembly on a flat surface. Use a framing square to make sure the jambs are perpendicular to the header, then attach temporary 1 × 2 cross braces at the bottom and both top corners (the braces keep the frame square and ensure that the frame is flush with the wall when the assembly is pulled into the door opening).

Continued next page

90° 90°

Dado joint reinforced with glue and woodscrews

Header

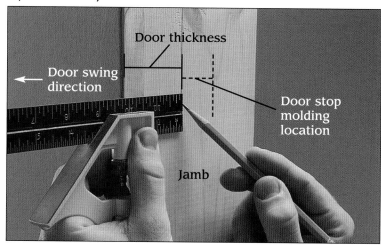

4 Draw reference lines on the jambs and header to mark locations for door stop molding. Mark the door thickness on the top and side members of the jamb using a combination square and measuring in from the jamb edges on the side of the door swing direction.

3 Set the frame into the door opening with the braces pulled flush against the wall. Install wood shims in the gaps between the jambs and the wall studs. Adjust the shims until the frame is level and plumb. Drive 8d casing (finish) nails through the jambs and into the wall studs at the shim locations (you should try to locate sets of shims at hinge locations, the door strike plate locations and the tops and bottoms of the jambs). Double-check to make sure the frame is still level and plumb, then trim off the ends of the shims with a hand saw.

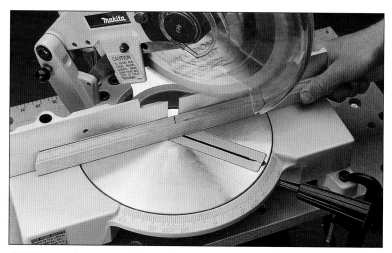

5 Miter-cut door stop molding to fit inside the door frame. Cut the molding with the broader edge—not the molded edge—against the saw fence.

6 Lay out hinge locations on the door jamb. For interior doors, two 3-in. butt hinges are usually enough to hold the door. The top of the upper hinge should be about 9 in. down from the header. The bottom of the lower hinge should be about 10 in. up from the floor. If you add a third hinge, center it between the upper and lower hinges. The depth of the mortise should equal the thickness of a hinge leaf. The mortises should

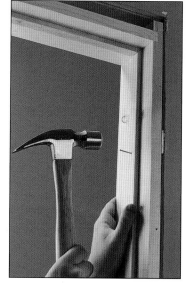

7 Nail the stop molding in place with 4d finish nails spaced about 12 in. apart. Be sure the molding aligns with the reference lines penciled on the jamb.

start 1/8 to 1/4 in. outside the stop molding reference line. Outline the hinge leaves at the correct locations, and remove waste wood with a chisel. Cut the outlines of the hinge leaf, then make repeated cuts across the face of the mortise about every 1/4 in. Pare away the waste with the chisel (bevel facing up), working from the jamb edge across the mortise face.

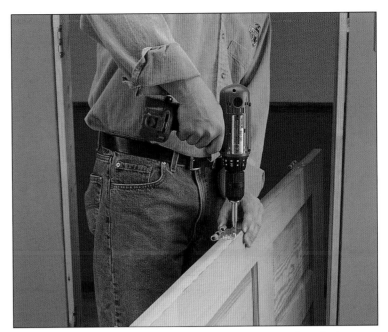

8 Set the door in the opening and prop it up on shims so there is a 1/8-in. gap between the door and frame on all sides. Mark the top and bottom of each hinge plate onto the face of the door. After removing the door, extend the marks onto the edge of the door and chisel mortises for the hinge leaves, as you did for the mortises on the jambs.

9 Attach the hinge plates to the door (remove the hinge pins from the hinges first, if they are the removable type). Drive only one screw per hinge plate, then test the operation by installing the door in the door opening. If the hinges are misaligned or the door is not square in the frame, adjust the mortise depth or height to compensate until everything is aligned and working smoothly. Then attach the hinges permanently by driving in the remaining hinge plate screws.

10 Hang the door in the frame, slipping shims underneath the door for support. Install the hinge pins and check the gap between the door and the jamb—it should be about 1/8 in. all the way around the door.

11 (Right) Install a door lockset and apply the finish before adding case molding trim.

TEST ONE

Plumb framing check (Photo left). Check the wall framing for plumb by holding a long level vertically against the stud edges and reading the bubble vials that are oriented horizontally (there should be one on each end of the level). If the wall studs are just slightly off plumb, you may be able to correct the problem by driving the sole plate with a hammer (Photo above).

TEST TWO

Crowned framing check. Use a long straightedge to test exposed wall studs for crowning before you install wallboard and trim. Be on the lookout for framing members that "crown" outward toward the room more than ¼ in.

Preparing walls & framing for trim installation

The best time to correct wall framing problems is before the wallboard is installed. If you're doing the framing work yourself, this won't be a problem. However, chances are you'll be installing trim over walls that are already finished past the drywall stage, which makes it much more difficult to correct wall framing problems. If your walls are still at the rough framing stage, here are a few preliminary checks to make:

Check wall framing for flatness and plumb. Take the longest level you've got or a 6 or 7-ft. strip of plywood with a flat edge and hold it vertically against the edges of each wall stud. Then make the same check holding the straightedge horizontally, perpendicular to the studs. Ideally, wall studs should be within ⅛ to ¼ in. of flat from floor to ceiling. Deflection along the edge of a stud is called crowning, and it's a common defect, especially in studs that aren't kiln dried. Severely crowned studs will distort the wallboard once it's hung, resulting in wavy wall surfaces. Be most concerned with the jack and king studs, as well as the first two or three studs on either side of a window or door opening beyond the king studs. These are the ones that will affect the flatness of the wallboard and in

---

Plumb, square and level

Establishing *plumb, square* and *level* is what trim carpentry is all about. The closer walls, windows, doors and ceilings are to being plumb, square and level, the easier the trimming tasks become. Here's what these terms mean: "Level" refers to an imaginary plane at any height that is parallel to the earth's surface. "Plumb" represents a straight plane or line perpendicular to the earth's surface. "Square" means that two planes or lines meet at a 90° angle. These geometric relationships are significant in trim carpentry. If, for instance, a door's side jamb is plumb and the head jamb is level, the corner formed by the two jamb pieces is square.

---

turn, the fit of the trim. Wall studs that crown away from the wall surface you'll be working on are less of a problem than those that crown toward you, especially if there are only a few bad ones interspersed among numbers of flat studs.

If you find a stud that deflects more than about ¼ in., there are a couple possible fixes you can try. For studs that crown toward you, an old carpenter's trick is to make a cut three-quarters of the way across the width of the offending stud and all the way through its thickness where it crowns the most. Make the cut straight and at a slight downward angle, starting from

How to Correct Convex Crowning

1 If a wall stud crowns outward in a convex shape, first find the point of maximum crowning. Then, make a downward angled kerf cut about ¾ of the way through the stud with a reciprocating saw or circular saw.

2 Drive a screw up through the kerf to draw the opposite sides of the kerf together. The thickness of the kerf will determine how much crowning is eliminated with this technique.

How to Correct Concave Crowning

1 If a wall stud crowns inward in a concave shape, make an angled kerf cut at the point of maximum crowning, as in Step 1 above. But instead of drawing the sides of the kerf together, spread them apart by driving shims into the kerf. Drive a shim from each direction to equalize the pressure in the kerf.

2 Break off the ends of the shims with a hammer, then reinforce the stud by attaching a scab board across the repair area. Use plywood to make the scab board, and attach it with screws and construction adhesive. Make sure it does not extend past the front edge of the stud.

the edge facing you. Then drive a long drywall or deck screw through this edge of the stud and up at an angle so it crosses the saw kerf about midway and keeps on going, forming an imaginary "X" with the kerf. Tightening the screw will close the saw kerf and flatten the crown somewhat. The wider the kerf, the more the stud will flatten when the kerf closes. If the stud crowns away from you, drive a pair of shims into the kerf to widen it, which will pull the stud back in your direction. Once you've flattened the stud by kerfing it, screw a plywood plate over the stud face in the repair area to lock the stud in position and reinforce the break. Another option for flattening a crown is simply to shave off the crowned area with a hand plane. Mark

Testing the Rough Opening

A rough opening should be square: the header and sill plate (in window openings) should be level, and the jack and king studs need to be plumb. Check for squareness by measuring opposite diagonals in the opening. If the diagonal measurements match, the opening is square. If not, you'll need to make adjustments by shimming or driving the framing members with a hammer.

Correcting Framing Errors

Pare back jambs that extend past the surface of the wallcovering. A low angle block plane is a good tool for this job.

Trim back framing members that are not flush. If you have access, use a block plane. In tighter areas, a chisel may work better.

a plumb reference line on the stud face near the front edge so you'll know how much material to remove.

Check the wall framing for plumb by holding a long level vertically against the stud edges and reading the bubble vials that are oriented horizontally (there should be one on each end of the level). If both bubbles aren't centered in the vials, tip the level away from the wall one end at a time until the bubbles center, to see which way the wall is leaning and by how much. You can also hang a plumb bob from a nail tacked into the edge of the wall's top plate between two studs. The point of the bob should align with the front edge of the sole plate if the wall is plumb. As a corrective measure, you may be able to whack the sole plate with a hammer to shift the wall into plumb, but more likely you'll need to pull out the nails that anchor the sole plate to the subfloor and tap the sole plate one way or the other to move the wall into plumb, then renail.

Check the rough openings for plumb, level and square. Set a level vertically along the face of one jack stud and another level along the bottom edge of the rough header. If the jack stud is plumb and the header is level, this corner of the opening is square. Measure across the opening from the plumb jack to the other jack at several points along the opening. If the measurements are equal, the other jack stud is plumb as well. You can also check for square by measuring diagonally from corner to corner across the opening. If the two diagonal measurements are equal, the opening is square. While you are checking for plumb and level, be sure the faces of the framing members are reasonably flat as well.

Since rough openings are oversized to begin with, as long as the rough opening doesn't deviate from plumb by more than about ¼ in. every 4 ft., or more than ½ in. out of square, don't bother to make adjustments to the rough opening. To shift a door jack stud into plumb, drive shims every 6 in. or so between it and the king stud in the area that falls out of plumb. Then, secure the shims by screwing or nailing through the jack stud and shim, and into the king stud. It's difficult to shim window jack studs into plumb without removing and shortening the rough sill first. If a header or rough sill are grossly out of level, you may be able to bring them into level by paring away the bottom edge of the header or the top face of the rough sill with a chisel as needed. It's more important for the header and sill to be square with the jack studs than level.

Check the wall to see that the edges of all the framing members are flush with one another. Mismatched framing joints will produce bulges in the wallboard, and these will affect how well the trim lays flat against the wall. Pare down any protruding wood with a hand plane or a chisel to flatten the framing joints, especially in the rough opening area.

Wallboard and jambs

If the window and door jambs and wallboard are already installed, inspect the area where the wallboard meets the jambs. Take the metal rule of your combination square and hold it on edge so it crosses the jamb edge and extends 6 in. or so onto the adjacent wallboard. Slide the straightedge all around the opening, checking for gaps. The edges of the jamb should be flush with the wallboard, but this is often not the case. Take note of where the wallboard and jamb deviate from one another by more than about ⅛ in. These are the areas to fix. Discrepancies of less than ⅛ in. aren't worth worrying about, especially if the case molding that you'll be installing has a recessed area on the back side. The molding should be able to bridge areas where the wallboard and jamb are only slightly out of alignment.

When the wallboard protrudes past the jamb edge, push on the wallboard to see if it gives a bit. Then try to flatten the wallboard against the framing where it protrudes past the jamb edge by driving a few screws through the wallboard and into the jack stud. If this doesn't do the trick, the next best method is to score through the surface paper with a utility knife in a crosshatch pattern, then shave the wallboard flush to the jamb edge with a rasp or Surform plane. An old chisel will also do the trick. You may discover that what you are paring away isn't actually wallboard but wallboard compound

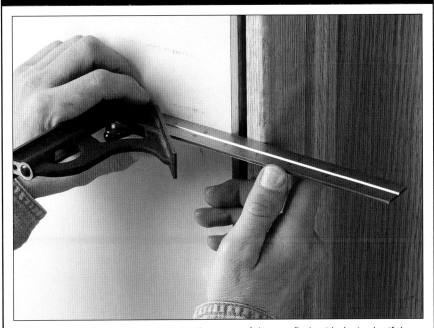

Check wallcoverings with a straightedge to see if they are flush with the jambs. If the jambs extend past the wallcovering, see the tip on the lower left, previous page. If the wallcovering extends past the jamb, see the remedies below.

Remove wallcovering material with a rasp or Surform plane (shown above). Before starting, draw a reference line indicating the coverage area for the case molding. Do not scrape or plane beyond this line.

Minor unevenness in wallboard can be eliminated simply by pounding the edge of the wallboard with a hammer. Score lines in the wallboard within the case molding area first to prevent damage to the wallboard in the area that will be visible.

instead, which indicates that two sheets of wallboard are meeting at a seam. Be sure to confine your repair efforts to an area no wider than what you'll be able to hide with the door or window casing. A good precaution against going too far is to mark a pencil line parallel to the jamb and ¼ in. in from the outside edge of whatever width casing you'll use.

A quicker method for flattening wallboard next to the jamb is to simply tap the wallboard with a hammer instead of shaving it. Tap lightly to crush the gypsum inside the wallboard but not so hard that you break through the surface paper. Tap until the wallboard face lines up with the jamb edge.

If the jamb edge stands proud of the wallboard, pull out your sharp hand or block plane and shave the jamb edge until it is flush with the wall. Be careful to feather out the area you plane so you don't create a noticeable dip along the edge of the jamb in the repair area. The object here is to keep the jamb edge as flat as possible over its length so the moldings will lay flat.

Jamb extensions

In cases where the jamb edges are set in from the wall by more than ⅛ in., you'll need to build out the jamb edges with strips of wood, called jamb extensions, to create a flush fit with the wall. The most common time you'll need to do this is if a window or door fitted with 4-in.-wide jambs is installed in a 2 × 6 stud wall. For windows cased picture-frame style, you'll need to add extensions along all four pieces of the jamb, including the sill. For windows that have a stool, the stool will serve as the sill jamb extension instead. Doors will need extension strips on the side and head jambs.

To create a jamb extension strip, select a board of the same thickness, length and wood type as the jamb edge you are working on, and place a flat edge of the board against the jamb edge. Scribe a

pencil line along the board with the pencil held flush against the wallboard. When you do this, the extension strip may extend the full length of the jamb edge or taper off at some point, which indicates that the jamb isn't plumb in the rough opening. Then trim the board along the pencil line with a jig saw to cut out the jamb extension strip, and glue the extension to the jamb edge. Hold each extension on the jamb with finish nails tacked in place until the glue dries. Then pull out the nails. Trim off any glue squeeze-out on the inside face of the jamb with a sharp chisel or utility knife.

Aside from correcting misalignments between jambs and walls, be sure to also check jambs for square. Measuring the diagonals or checking the corners with a framing square are the quickest methods for making these checks. If the jambs are more than ¼ in. out of square, it will affect trim joints.

MAKING JAMB EXTENSIONS

1 Select boards that are the same species and thickness as the jambs. Cut them to length. Hold each board flush against the jamb and scribe a cutting line that follows the wallcovering.

OPTION: PREASSEMBLED JAMB EXTENSION UNIT

Stool extension

1 Especially when extending 4-in.-wide jambs to fit into a 2 × 6 stud wall, consider building a complete jamb extension frame in your shop, then installing the unit whole into the window or door opening. First, measure the precise distances between the existing jambs to determine the dimensions of the new unit. Add ¼ in. to each dimension—this will create a ⅛ in. reveal at each edge, giving you a small margin for error when installing the unit. Use stock that's the same species and thickness as the jamb to make the jamb extension members. Assemble the frame with glues and screws. For windows (except when using picture-frame casing on all sides) make and attach a stool extension.

2 Clamp the workpiece to your worksurface. Then, carefully trim along the scribed cutting line with a jig saw. Use a jig saw blade with a high tooth-per-inch count (10 to 14 tpi) to get a smoother cut.

3 Drill pilot holes then attach the jamb extensions with finish nails long enough to extend at least 1 in. into the jamb. Wood glue is also recommended to keep the joint tight.

2 (ABOVE) Check the unit to make sure it's square, then test-fit it into the window or door opening. Make adjustments as needed, then attach the case molding to the jamb extension unit.

3 (RIGHT) Set the unit into the opening so the back edges are flush against the jambs and the case molding is pressed against the wall. Adjust its position so the reveal is even on all sides where the extension meets the old jambs. Drive 8d casing nails through the case molding and into the framing members of the rough opening to install the unit. Also drive nails through the extension jambs and into the rough opening framing members.

Case molding

Over the years, architects and carpenters have established a number of conventional schemes for applying casing to doors and windows. It's common practice for doors and windows in the same room to have complementary if not matching trim schemes. By trim scheme, we mean the style and configuration of the moldings used, as well as how the moldings fit together in the corners.

Door and window trim is made up of three principal parts: a *head casing* that covers the edge of the head jamb and two *side casings* that cover the side jambs. Doors have no casing covering the sill, of course, but sill jambs on windows can be trimmed with either a stool and apron or plain sill casing.

For windows and doors, a trim scheme can be made up of more than just three or four parts, depending on how elaborate and fanciful you want to get. Following are the most common window and door casing schemes you'll find in today's homes.

Window casing

Picture-frame casing. As the name implies, windows cased in this scheme look like they are mounted in picture frames. Instead of a stool and apron covering the sill jamb, it is concealed with a piece of sill casing that matches the side and head casings. The four strips of molding form 45° miters in the corners—or very close to 45°, depending on how square the jambs are. Moldings with simpler profiles, like ranch molding, are generally used for picture-frame schemes. Since there's nothing hiding the miter joints, the moldings must meet tightly in the corners.

Careful, precise installation of the case molding puts a professional finishing touch on window and door trim—and can even conceal minor errors.

Common case molding types

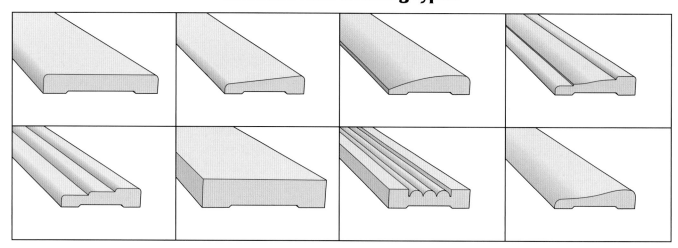

A variety of profiles gives you many options when choosing premilled case molding. From simple ranch molding to fluted trim boards, just about any kind of trim will work. Most of the standard profiles shown above are in the 2-to-3-in. wide range.

Mitered casing with stool and apron. Head and side casings in this scheme form 45° miter joints in the corners, picture-frame style. The side casings, however, butt squarely against a flat stool that either fits against the edge of the sill jamb or overlaps it. The profiles on the head and side casings match. Generally, the molding profile for the casing has a more intricate and interesting profile than the picture-frame scheme, and the molding width is 2½ in. or less. A strip of molding called an *apron* is nailed to the wall beneath the stool. The apron may be made of the same molding as the head and side casings, or it may simply be a flat strip with the ends trimmed square, mitered or with a coped profile that matches the face profile. Usually the ends of the apron align with the outside edges of the side casings.

Butted casing with stool and apron. This style takes on more variations than any of the other window casing schemes. In simplest form, the side and head casings are the same thickness, and they form butt joints where they meet in the corners. Depending on architectural style, the side casings may be the same width or narrower than the head casing. The head casing may be thicker than the side casings. The casings may be flat, profiled or decorated with a series of parallel flutes. The ends of the head casing may align with the outside edges of the side casings or extend past them by as much as an inch or more. The head and side casings may be enhanced by adding a few more moldings to them, or by installing decorative corner blocks where the head and side casings meet.

Stool and apron with no casing. A more contemporary approach usually reserved for windows made of vinyl or metal, this trim scheme involves wrapping part or all of the inside window jamb with wallboard rather than casing. Windows trimmed this way often have a

Window casing schemes

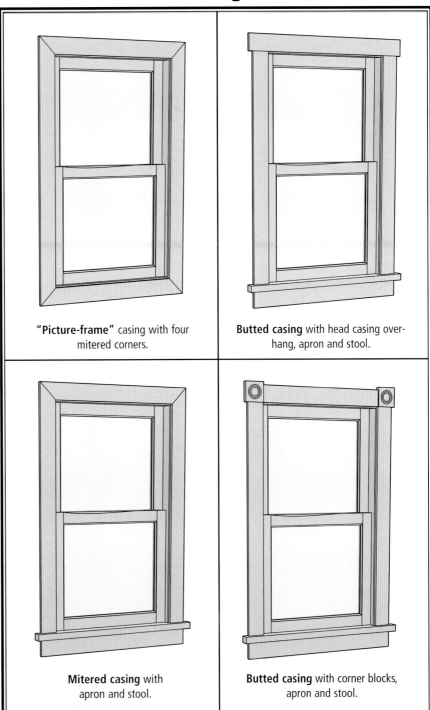

"Picture-frame" casing with four mitered corners.

Butted casing with head casing overhang, apron and stool.

Mitered casing with apron and stool.

Butted casing with corner blocks, apron and stool.

stool that may be made of wood or another material such as cultured marble. There may or may not be an apron beneath the stool.

Door casing

Mitered casing. In rooms where the window casing is mitered, the doors will be outfitted with mitered casing also. Head and side casings meet in 45° miters, and the side casings butt against the floor.

Butted casing. This scheme is the door counterpart to stool-and-apron windows trimmed with butted casings. If the baseboard in the room is the same thickness as the side and head casings of doors

Door casing schemes

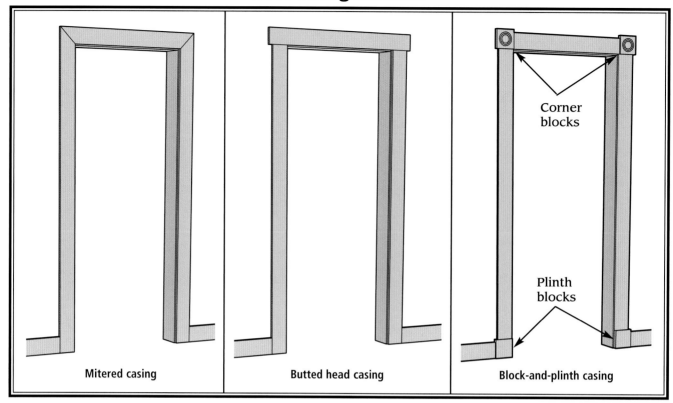

Mitered casing

Butted head casing

Block-and-plinth casing

Corner blocks

Plinth blocks

trimmed this way, a strip of back-band molding may wrap around the outside edges of the door casing all the way around to create a decorative reveal where the baseboard butts against the door casing (See page 68).

Blocked casing. Instead of meeting in miter or butt joints, the side and head casings butt against thicker corner blocks, which often are milled with a decorative rosette or bullseye pattern. The side casings may extend all the way to the floor or stop short, butting against another pair of blocks (called plinth blocks) at the floor. Plinth blocks are thicker than both the case molding and the baseboard. If the doors in a room are blocked, the windows often will have decorative corner blocks as well, located between the head and side casings.

Door casing kits

Instead of purchasing lengths of case molding for trimming an interior door, you can buy prepackaged door trim kits that include all the moldings you'll need to complete the job. Kits are available for casing a door picture-frame style, and the miters are already precut on the head and side casings. You can also find kits for installing butted casings that include corner and plinth blocks. Whichever kit style you choose, it will be sized according to the industry nomenclature for door width sizes. Each different width is represented by two numerals separated by a slash: 2/0, 2/4, 2/6, 2/8 and 3/0. The first numeral in the code represents feet and the second numeral is inches. A 2/6 door, for example, means the door is 2 ft. 6 in. wide, or 30 in. Be sure to buy the kit that matches your door width. The side casings in the kit are cut long; trim them to length to fit your door.

Installing mitered window casing

Ask several different trim carpenters how they install picture-frame casing, and you'll probably get several different answers about which piece to nail first. Some prefer to measure, cut and fasten the side casings first, then cut and fit the head casing followed by the sill casing. Others work clockwise around the window starting with the head casing. Most trim carpenters work from the top down, cutting and nailing the head casing first, then cutting and fitting both side casings to the head casing and finishing up with the sill casing. We'll use the last method for the installation sequence shown here. Whichever method you choose, be fussy about the fit of the miters, especially the two at the ends of the head casing—they're the most noticeable.

Mitered casing is the most popular window and door trim scheme today. Sometimes called "picture window" casing, the casing can be installed with simple miter joints at all corners, or with butt joints at a sill or the floor (on a door).

Calculating mitered casing length

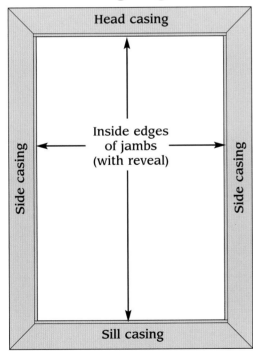

The surest way to get a good fit with mitered case molding is to position each piece on the opening, measure for the reveal from the inside edges of the jambs, then transfer the positions onto the workpiece. But if you need or prefer to measure and mark, simply measure the distance between the inside edges of opposing jambs then add twice the reveal width to get the short measurement on mitered casing.

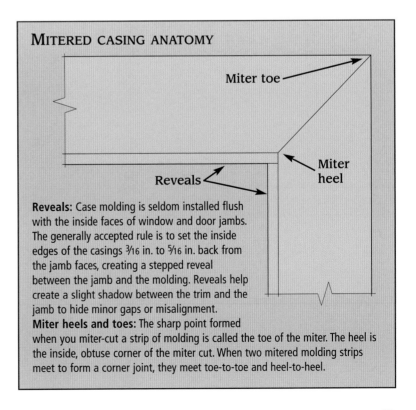

MITERED CASING ANATOMY

Reveals: Case molding is seldom installed flush with the inside faces of window and door jambs. The generally accepted rule is to set the inside edges of the casings 3/16 in. to 5/16 in. back from the jamb faces, creating a stepped reveal between the jamb and the molding. Reveals help create a slight shadow between the trim and the jamb to hide minor gaps or misalignment.

Miter heels and toes: The sharp point formed when you miter-cut a strip of molding is called the toe of the miter. The heel is the inside, obtuse corner of the miter cut. When two mitered molding strips meet to form a corner joint, they meet toe-to-toe and heel-to-heel.

1 Mark a trim reveal all around the jamb. A typical width for reveals is 3/16 in. These reveal lines will serve as alignment aids for positioning the corners and inside edges of the casing. To make the reveal, set the end of a combination square blade 3/16 in. from the head of the tool, and hold a pencil against the blade end as you guide the square around the inside faces of the jamb to mark the jamb edges. Be sure to lay out the corners of the jamb with reveal lines to indicate precisely where the inside edges of the casing will meet.

TIP: Make a gauge for setting consistent reveals. Cut rabbets on all four edges of a square block of wood. The width of the rabbets should correspond to common reveal widths. Hold the gauge against the inside edge of the jamb and slide it along the edge, tracing with a pencil as you go.

2 Cross-cut the head, side and sill casing pieces to rough length. Cut the strips long enough to account for the miter cuts plus a little extra for good measure (See "Calculating mitered casing length," previous page). Mark and cut the head casing to length. Miter-cut one end of the head to 45°. Set the head casing in place so the heel (the inside corner) of this miter intersects with the corner reveal marks on the jamb. Adjust the casing so it aligns with the rest of the reveal marks on the head jamb, and mark the other end of the molding at the corner reveal marks. Miter-cut this end of the casing to cut the head casing to final length.

3 Attach the head casing to the jamb first, then the header. Hold the head casing in position on the jamb and drive a 3d or 4d finish nail through the head casing about 3/16 in. from the inside edge. Center this first nail roughly along the length of the molding. Then, nail the casing to the jamb out from the center in both directions with more nails of the same gauge. Space the nails about every 8 in. Stop the outermost nails at least 1 in. in from the ends of the casing to keep from splitting the wood at the miters. Be sure the casing aligns with the reveal marks as you nail, and that both miter heels intersect the corner reveal marks. Now that the inside edge of the casing is fastened to the jamb, secure the outer edge by driving 6d or 8d nails through the casing and into the header. Locate these nails about 3/16 in. in from the top edge of the head casing and opposite each short nail you drove into the jamb.

CLOSING MITERED CASING GAPS

Even gap

Open heel

Open toe

Often, miter joints don't align correctly on the first try, so here are a few corrective measures you can make to improve the fit: First, align the side casing so it follows the reveal marks. If there's an **even gap** from toe to heel, then the back edges of the joint are touching, but not the front edges. Correct the problem by removing 1/32 in. or so of material along the back edge of the miter from toe to heel to draw

the front edges of the joint together. Trim with a sharp block plane, chisel, file or on the power miter saw. If the toes touch but not the heels **(open heel)**, trim a few shavings off the miter toe, tapering the cut down to the miter heel. If the miter heels touch but the toes open up **(open toe)**, trim 1/32 in. or so from heel of the side casing, tapering the cut up to, but not shortening, the miter toe.

4 Miter-cut the tops of the side casings and fit them against the head casing. If the miter joints meet evenly and without gaps and the inside edge of the side casing parallels the reveal marks, then mark and cut the bottom miters on the side casings. (If the joint isn't clean, see the suggestions above.) Mark the side casings to length where they intersect the bottom corner reveals, and miter-cut the bottoms of the side casings at 45°.

5 Attach the side casings to the side jambs and jack studs, just as you attached the head casing. Before nailing the moldings in place, spread glue along the mitered top ends of the side casings as well as the ends of the head casing. Glue will help hold the joint together, but it also will slow down the rate that the end grain absorbs moisture, which can cause the miter joints to open up.

6 Nail the side casings first on the jamb side, then to the jack studs. Stop nailing about 1 ft. from the bottom ends of the casing pieces, so these ends can flex in or out in relation to the sill casing for making the final fit.

Continued next page

7 Cut the sill casing to length. First, miter-cut one end of the sill molding to 45°. Set the sill casing upside down and against the miter toes of the side casings, with the miter toe of the sill casing touching the miter toe of the side casing. Mark the overall length of the sill casing where it intersects the other side casing miter toe.

8 Cut this second 45° miter 1/16 in. outside the mark you just made, and test the fit of the sill casing between the side casing pieces.

Cut second miter so trim piece is slightly long

9 Trim a little bit of material off the trim piece at the second miter, using your miter saw. Check the fit again (Step 8). Continue trimming tiny amounts of material from the trim until the miter fit is perfect and the moldings follow the reveal lines.

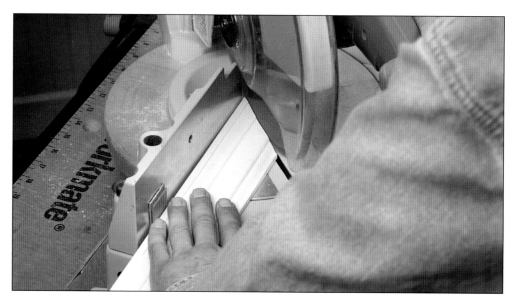

10 Spread glue on the mating edges of the bottom miter joints, and nail the sill casing and the unnailed bottom portions of the side casings in place.

11 Lock the miter joints with 2d or 3d finish nails. As a precautionary measure against future gaps developing in the miter joints, drive a nail through the outside edge of the side casings or the top edge of the head casing at an angle across the miters. If you are nailing by hand rather than with a pneumatic nailer, tap these nails home carefully to keep from splitting the molding or marring the wall. A good safeguard against splits is to drill pilot holes for the nails using a 2d nail chucked in your drill. Then lay a piece of cardboard against the wall in the nailing area to act as a shield when you drive the nails.

12 Drive a 2d or 3d finish nail into the pilot hole to lock each miter joint. Flatten any mismatches along the faces of the miter joints with a sharp chisel. Recess the nailheads with a nailset and fill the holes with color-matched wood putty or putty stick.

Mitered door casing terminates at the bottom with a butt joint at the floor or at the top of a plinth block.

Installing mitered door casing

Trimming doors with mitered casing is much the same process as trimming windows picture-frame style (See pages 54 to 57). Reserve mitered door casing for moldings that are profiled rather than flat. If the head and side casings are flat across the face, install them with butt joints instead.

The procedure for trimming doors with mitered casing is to start with the head casing, then move to both side casings, finessing the top miter joints for a tight fit. You could install the side casings first, but if the top miters are even slightly out of alignment with one another, it will be far more difficult to cut and fit the head casing miters.

1 Mark the head and side jambs for an even casing reveal. As for windows, door casing usually is set back 3/16 in. from the inside face of the jamb. Mark the reveals using an reveal gauge with a 3/16-in. rabbet or a combination square with the blade set to 3/16 in. (See page 54). Be sure to mark the corners of the jamb where the head and side casings intersect. Cut the head casing to length. Start with a length of casing about 1 in. longer than needed (See "Calculating mitered casing length," page 53). Miter-cut one end of the molding to 45°. Hold the head casing against the head jamb and so the heel of the miter is aligned with the corner reveal marks. Shift the casing up or down slightly as needed so the inside edge follows the head casing reveal marks, then mark the other miter heel at the opposite corner reveal marks. Miter-cut this end at 45°.

2 Nail the head casing in place. Fasten the casing first to the head jamb, starting at the center and nailing out to the ends of the molding with 3d or 4d finish nails, set back from the inside edge of the molding about 3/16 in. Stop nailing about 1 in. from the ends of the head casing to keep from splitting through to the miters. Space the nails every 8 to 10 in. Then drive 6d or 8d nails through the face of the molding near the top edge to secure it to the header framing. Use the same nail spacing and align the larger nails with the smaller nails across the molding.

3 Cut the side casing to rough length. Measure from the finished floor along the side jambs to the miter toes of the head casing, and add ½ in. for waste. Cut two strips of casing to this length. Crosscut the bottom ends square, but miter-cut the top ends at 45°. Check the fit of the miter joints. Set each side casing in place against the head casing. Since the side casings are slightly longer than needed, the bottoms of the molding pieces will bow away at the floor. The inside edges of the casing should follow the side jamb reveal lines, and the miter joints should close tightly. If the casing overlaps the reveals when you hold the miter joint closed, use a sharp block plane and trim off a few shavings from the toe of the miter. Trim from the miter heel if the molding drifts away from the reveals.

4 Cut the side casings to length. Once the miter joints close and the casings follow the reveals, flip each strip end-for-end so the miter toe touches the floor. Set the molding in place against the jamb and mark it where the outside edge of the side casing intersects the top edge of the head casing. Crosscut the side casings ¹/₁₆ in. longer than this measurement for a tight fit to the floor. NOTE: If the flooring you measured from isn't the final flooring, slip a piece of the final flooring between the side casings and the subfloor when you mark the casings for length. For floors that will be carpeted, measure the casing length from the existing flooring, then subtract ¼ in. to allow for the carpet thickness.

5 Fasten the side casings to the side jambs, then to the jack studs. First, spread glue along the miters. Secure the casing to the side jambs, driving 3d or 4d nails through the face of the side casings about ³/₁₆ in. from the inside edge and into the side jambs. Nail along the full length of the molding. Keep the molding aligned with the reveals as you work. Use 6d or 8d nails to pin the outer edge of the side casings to the wall, driving the nails into the jack studs. Start nailing at the miter to hold it closed, working your way down toward the floor. Space nails about 12 in. apart, aligned in pairs across the width of the molding.

6 (Right) Lock the corner miter joints by driving a pair of 2d finish nails through the outside edges of the casings and across the joint. Drill pilot holes for these nails first, if possible, with a 2d nail chucked in a drill. Tap the nails carefully, and protect the wall surface in the nailing area with a scrap of cardboard to keep from marring the wall with the hammer.

7 (Left) Recess the nailheads with a nailset, and fill the nail holes with wood putty or putty stick. Pare back any slight mismatches in the miter with a sharp wood chisel.

Stool-and-apron casing

Installing stool-and-apron casing is the traditional method for trimming a window. If the window sill has a flat edge and the jamb is flush with the surrounding wall surface, installing a stool is much like fastening the sill casing in a picture-frame trimming job. Once you determine and cut the stool to length, it's really just a matter of gluing the stool to the front edge of the sill and nailing it with long finish nails. In newer construction, however, it's common for walls to be framed with 2 × 6s instead of 2 × 4s, so the window sill and jambs aren't wide enough to be flush with the wall surface. In these instances, the stool must be scribed and cut so it can extend into the window opening and meet the sill. You'll also need to scribe and cut the stool if the sill is angled so the stool can fit over the back edge of the sill.

Stools and aprons are common details on older double-hung windows, and they continue to be installed on modern, energy efficient windows to lend a traditional accent. Stools on old windows serve a couple of functions: they overlap and hide the back edge of the jamb sill, and they seal the front bottom edge of the lower window sash when it's closed to keep moisture and drafts out. Years ago, all windows were manufactured with sills that sloped away from the interior side of the window to help shed water. An angled rabbet on the bottom back edge of the stool allowed it to fit over the top back edge of the angled sill but still form a level, flat surface inside the building.

Windows with a stool and apron usually are cased with butt joints at the head casing as well as the stool.

Stool horn options

Square-cut horn

Beveled horn

Some window manufacturers still outfit windows with sloping sills, but more and more new windows have a flat front sill edge to make installing a stool or sill casing for picture-frame applications easier. Depending on the manufacturer, some windows with flat sills will have a groove milled along the front edge to accept a stool outfitted with a tongue.

The ends of a stool, called the *horns,* overlap the side jambs and project out past the outside edges of the side casings. The horns provide a base for butting the bottom ends of the side casings. Beyond this practical purpose, the horns serve mostly as decoration, helping to visually "anchor" the window to the wall and balance the window trim top-to-bottom.

The apron, which butts against the bottom of the stool, hides the gap where the wall surface ends along the top edge of the rough sill. Generally, aprons are made from the same case molding used on the side and head casings. The apron length matches the width of the side casings measured from outside edge to outside edge.

Regardless of whether you'll trim the side and head jambs of a stool-and-apron window with mitered or butted case moldings, start by installing the stool and apron, then proceed up the jamb, nailing the side casings and then the head casing.

Stools are available in both stain and paint grades, but you may have to special-order them from your local building center. Lumberyards that cater to contractors probably will have stools in stock. Stools come in standard widths and lengths to fit common window sizes or in longer pieces that you cut to length. Most

Apron styles

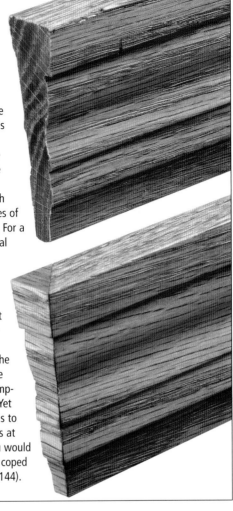

Apron molding can be finished on the ends in several ways. The easiest method is simply to cut it square, as in the top photo to the right (the ends should align with the outside edges of the side casing). For a more professional look, bevel the ends and cut beveled return pieces to form beveled joints at the outside corners, as in the bottom photo. The return pieces are attached by clamping and gluing. Yet another option is to make coped cuts at the ends, as you would when making a coped joint (See page 144).

Mitered return horn

Roundover horn

Stool styles

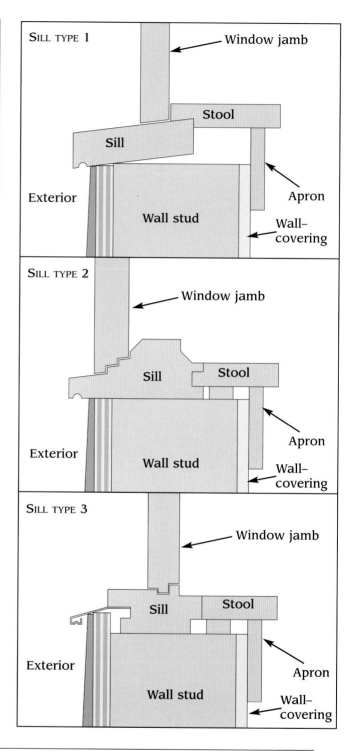

Sill type 1
Window jamb
Stool
Sill
Exterior
Apron
Wall stud
Wall–covering

Sill type 2
Window jamb
Sill
Stool
Apron
Exterior
Wall stud
Wall–covering

Sill type 3
Window jamb
Sill
Stool
Exterior
Apron
Wall stud
Wall–covering

Premilled window stool moldings come in a number of profiles and styles. The choice of which to use should factor in both structural and aesthetic requirements. Before choosing, inspect the window sill. If it is beveled (See Sill type 1 illustration above), you'll want to choose a stool that has a wide, angled rabbet groove on the underside, as with the upper two types pictured above. The rabbet fits over the edge of the sill, following its angle to create a level surface. If your sill has a groove in the edge (See Sill type 2 illustration above), look for a stool with a premilled tongue to fit into the groove. If the sill is square and level (See Sill type 3 illustration above), you can use plain stool molding, as pictured in the bottom of the photo above.

stools still are made with an angled rabbet in the bottom back edge for installing over sloped sills, but you also can find stool stock with a flat back edge or outfitted with a tongue for fitting against flat-sill windows. Stools are milled with several different profiles along their front edges, so choose the one you like. Buy a stool that's wide enough to project from the sill out over the apron and form an overhang of at least ½ in. If the jambs of the windows you are trimming are flush with the surrounding wall surface, it's easy to deter-

mine the width you need. Simply measure the stool from the deepest part of the angled rabbet (or the flat back edge if the stool has no angled rabbet) out to the front profiled edge. Then subtract the thickness of your apron casing from this measurement to determine the overhang you'll get if you use this width of stool. Also, buy a stool long enough to create overhangs beyond the outside edges of the side casings and the ends of the apron.

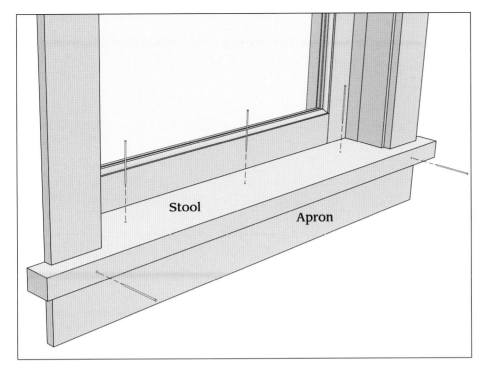

Nailing a stool

To attach a stool to a window frame, nail through the front edge of the stool and into the studs on the sides of the rough opening. Drill pilot holes first to prevent splitting the stool. Also drive long finish nails (8d or so) down through the stool and into the rough sill. For stools with horns measuring 3 in. and longer, fasten the horns to the wall with 8d finish nails driven through the front edge of the horn and into the jack stud.

HOW TO INSTALL A STOOL & APRON

1 Determine the amount the stool will overhang the apron once it is installed. Calculate this overhang by measuring out from the edge of the sill to the wall surface and adding the thickness of the apron piece to this distance. If you are installing a stool over an angled sill, add the width of the angled rabbet on the bottom of the stool to the total. Subtract this overall measurement from the width of the stool. The difference equals the amount the stool will overhang the apron.

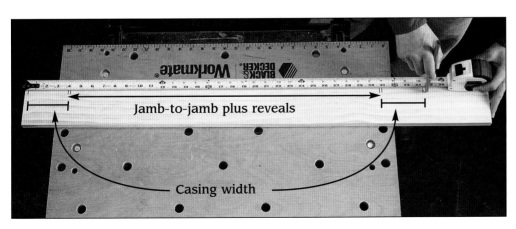

2 Cut the stool stock a few inches longer than rough finished length. Lay out cutting lines for the final length onto the stock. Include marks for the jamb-to-jamb measurement, plus both reveals, as well as the casing widths and the casing overhang, if any. Cut the stool to length.

Continued next page

3 Mark the horn lengths on the stool. First, find and mark the centers of both the sill and stool, lengthwise. Hold the stool in place against the wall and even with the top of the sill. Align the centerlines you just drew with a combination square held against the front edge of the stool. Then slide the combination square along the stool until the blade hits a jack stud (if the window jamb is recessed) or a side jamb. Scribe a line along the blade of the square across the stool to mark the face of the jack stud or side jamb. Duplicate this process to mark a reference line for the jack stud or side jamb on the other end of the stool.

4 Scribe the horns to width. Here's what to do if the sill is recessed in the wall opening: With the stool held in place on the wall, set a compass the distance from the edge of the sill to the back edge of the stool. If this distance varies across the width of the window, set the compass for the widest point.

5 With the compass point held against the wall, scribe a line out from each reference line you drew in Step 3 to the ends of the stool to establish the horn width. For windows with angled sills and flush jambs, set the compass to match the width of the angled rabbet that's milled into the bottom back edge of the stool, and use this compass setting for establishing the horn widths.

6 Trim the horns to shape with a jig saw. To allow for some adjustment when fitting the stool, cut just on the waste side of your horn layout lines with the saw base set for a slight back cut. This way, you'll be able to pare up to your layout lines later, if necessary, to improve the fit of the stool in the opening.

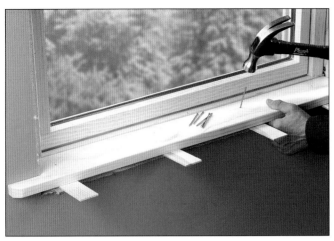

7 Fasten the stool in place. Be sure to first check that the stool is level across its width and along its length. If the jamb is recessed in the rough framing and not flush with the surrounding walls, first align the stool with the sill by slipping pairs of tapered shims or scraps of plywood beneath the stool and on top of the rough sill. It's common to leave a 1/8-in. reveal between the top edge of the flat sill and the top face of the stool, so you may not need to add much shimming. Spread wood glue along the back edge of the stool and the mating sill edge, set the stool in position on the shims and nail through the stool and shims into the rough sill with long finish nails. If the stool has an

angled rabbet that overlaps the sill, nail down through the stool and into the sill with 8d finish nails to secure the stool (Above, left). For flat-sill installations where the stool butts against the sill, drive three to five 16d finish nails through the front edge of the stool and into the sill (Above, right). To provide additional support, toe-nail 8d finish nails through the stool and into the sill. For stools with horns measuring 3 in. and longer, fasten the horns to the wall with 8d finish nails driven through the front edge of the horn and into the jack stud. OPTION: Hold the stool level by screwing a couple of thick wood scraps to the wall beneath the stool, to serve as temporary supports (Above, right).

8 Make the apron. Find the length of the apron by measuring the distance between the reveal marks on the side jambs, then adding twice the width of the side casings to this measurement. Cut the apron to size, choosing and using one of the end treatment methods discussed on page 73. Fasten the apron beneath the stool with 8d finish nails, driving the nails through the face of the apron and into the rough sill. Also drive a finish nail through the apron and into each jack stud in the rough opening. Center the apron lengthwise beneath the stool before fastening it in place so the ends of the apron will line up with the outside edges of the side casings, once they are installed.

9 Attach jamb extensions to the side and head jambs if they're not flush to the wall surface (See pages 48 to 49). Without flush jamb surfaces you can't proceed to install side and head casings. Cut the head jamb extension long enough to overlap the side jamb extensions, and install it first with glue and nails, driving nails through the extension and into the head jamb. Then measure, cut and install the side jamb extensions so they butt against the head jamb extension and the stool. When nailing the extension strips to the jamb, drive the nails near the outside edges of the extension strips so the nailheads won't show once the casings are installed. Drill pilot holes for the nails to keep them from splitting the extension strips or the sill, and use finish nails long enough to penetrate the sill by at least 3/4 in. Finally, mark the 3/16-in. casing reveals on the front edges of the side and head jamb extensions.

Installing butted casing over a window stool

You can case the side and head jambs of a stool-and-apron window picture-frame style, mitering the head and side casings and butting the side casings against the stool. For more on measuring and cutting mitered casing, see pages 53 to 57. But more often, stool-and-apron trimmed windows have butted head and side casings. Butted casings offer more detailing options, as you'll see on pages 68 to 69. Following is the process for installing case molding that butts up against a window stool.

HOW TO INSTALL BUTTED CASING OVER A STOOL

1 Cut the side casings to length. To determine their overall length, measure from the top of the stool along the side jambs and up to the head jamb reveal lines. Add an extra ½ in. for waste. Cross-cut one end of each side casing piece square and butt this end against the stool. Inspect how the inside edge of the casing follows the reveal marks on the jamb. If a casing wanders from the reveal marks, set a compass to ¼ in., shift the casing so it aligns with the reveals and scribe the casing where it meets the stool. Cut along the scribe line.

2 Once the casings meet the stool flush and follow the reveal marks, mark the top ends where the casing meets the head casing reveal marks. To do this, first tack the side casings temporarily to the jamb with a couple of finish nails. Hold a long level or straightedge across the window opening, aligned with the head casing reveal marks, and draw a cut line across each side casing. Cross-cut the casings to length along these cut lines.

3 Cut the bottoms of the side casings at a slight back bevel to bring the face-edge of the casing tight against the stool. The gap formed by the back bevel along the back edge of the casing won't be noticeable. To cut the back bevels, pivot your miter saw right or left about 2° off of square, and cut the side casings standing on edge against the saw fence. You can also leave the saw positioned for a square cut and lay the casing flat on the saw table. Insert a thin shim beneath the casing near the saw blade to raise the molding slightly off the saw table, and make the cut to form the back bevel.

4 (Left) Nail the side casings in place, first along the jambs, then into the jack studs. Arrange the nail placement in pairs across the width of the casing about every 12 in. Use 3d or 4d nails along the jamb and 6d or 8d nails for nailing the casings to the jack studs. Be sure to drill pilot holes for the nails, and check to make sure the casing is aligned with the reveal marks.

DESIGN OPTION:
Extend head casing

One of the advantages to butt joints between the head and side casing members is that you have some flexibility to build a little overhang into the head casing. The effect can be quite minimal, as with the project shown in this sequence, or more dramatic, as with the shed door casing above. Longer overhangs convey a more "rustic" feel.

5 Mark and cut the head casing. Depending on the window trim scheme you've chosen, the ends of the head casing can either be flush with the outside edges of the side casings or overhang them by some amount. It's common to make the head casing the same length as the stool. Butt the head casing against the top ends of the side casings, then nail it in place, first along the head jamb, then into the header framing. Start at the center of the head casing and nail out to the ends. If the head casing overhangs the outside edges of the side casings, be sure to adjust it for an even overhang before fastening. Use the same nail sizes as for the side casings when attaching the head casing to the head jamb and header. Recess all exposed nailheads with a nailset and conceal the holes with wood putty or putty stick.

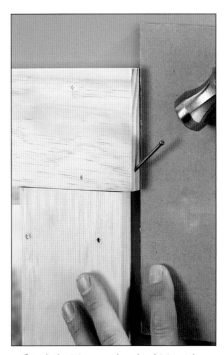

6 Lock the joints togehter by driving 3d nails through both joint members at an angle. Be sure to drill a pilot hole first.

THICKER HEAD CASING

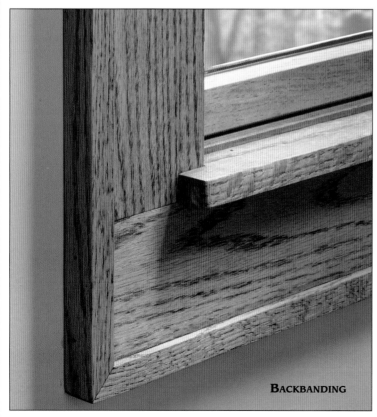

BACKBANDING

You can dress up your trim scheme by selecting case molding with an elegant profile, but there are other easy treatments you might want to consider instead. The four photographs on these pages represent a good sampling of these treatments. If you're interested in getting a little creative with your trim schemes, make sure to plan for it in advance—shifting gears in mid-project is very inefficient. And keep in mind that the effect is generally most successful when the same treatment is used on all of the windows and doors in the same room.

Thicker head casing

It's common to see butted head casings overhang the side casings, and you can enhance this design feature even more if you start with head casing stock that's thicker than the side casings. Thicker head casing creates a reveal where it meets the side casings and helps break up the single plane created by the faces of all the various casing pieces. Thicker head casings only make sense in butted casing schemes, and they look best with wider, flat casings. Aim for about 1/8 in. to 1/4 in. of reveal between the faces of the head and side casings.

Backbanding

Another way to hide the end grain of head casings on windows and doors is to wrap the outside edges of the side and head casings with "backband." Backband comes in a variety of profiles, and it's usually milled with a rabbet along the inside edge to fit like a cap over the edges of other moldings. Another visual advantage to backband is that it "builds out" the thickness of the case molding so that narrower moldings, like base molding, can butt against it and form a reveal. Install backband only if the side and head casing thickness is the same, and nail it in place after the side and head casings are installed as a final trim step. Miter-cut the joints where strips of backband meet in the corners.

Applied bead

Another way to make butted head casing look distinctive is to fasten a thin but wider strip of molding along the bottom edge of the head casing to act as a visual spacer between the head casing and the side casings. Applied bead usually projects out from the face of the head casing by about 1/4 in. and sometimes overhangs the ends of the head casing by the same amount. This isn't always the case, however. Sometimes the bead actually is narrower than the head casing thickness but wider than the side casing thickness, which creates a "stepped" reveal above and below the bead. The front edge and ends of the bead strip can be flat or profiled, and the thickness of this molding strip generally is about 1/4 in. to 5/16 in. Stop molding for door jambs can do double duty as applied bead. Stop molding comes in a number of different profiles, and the proportions of the molding are about right for 7/8-in.-thick head casing. To install a bead projection, mark and cut it to length and fasten it to the bottom edge of the head casing with glue and short brads. Then nail the head casing assembly in place on the jamb, butted against the side casings and flush with the head casing reveal marks.

"Cabinet" head casing

Cabinet heads, also called pediments, consist of a number of different molding strips applied to the head jamb to create a built-up, cornice effect. Cabinet heads look appropriate on windows and doors with butted head casings where the ends of the head casing are even with the outside edges of the side casings. Build a cabinet head before installing the head casing. This way, you can fit and install the moldings to the head casing while it's still at a comfortable working height. Then, nail the cabinet head assembly in place over the tops of the side casings, just as you would install the plain head casing.

APPLIED BEAD

"CABINET" HEAD CASING

Blocking. Installing blocking involves nailing decorative blocks in the corners where the side and head casings meet. Usually, corner blocks are about ⅛-in. thicker than the rest of the casing in order to create reveals at the casing joints. The reveals are both decorative and functional. If the faces of the head and side casings are at all misaligned with one another, the thicker corner blocks will hide the mismatch. You'll find premilled corner blocks in thicknesses of ⅞ in. and ⅝ in., sized to be used with ¾ and ½-in.-thick casing. Most are decorated with some form of relief carving— commonly bullseyes or rosettes.

Plinth blocks are installed between door side casing and the floor, generally in tandem with blocks at the top corners. Plinth blocks are usually thicker than corner blocks, as well as wider and taller than the rest of the standing or running casing in the room. The oversized proportions serve the same purpose as corner blocks, creating reveals at the side casing and baseboard joints. Manufactured plinth blocks usually have a profile milled along the top edge to mimic the basemolding. You can find them in a variety of sizes up to 6 × 8 in. or larger.

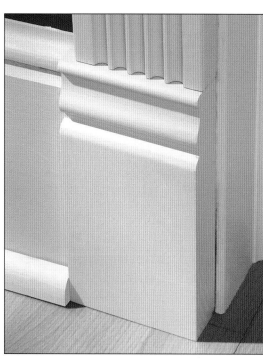

Block-and-plinth casing lends a bit of formality and visual interest to butted door casings—and it's very easy to install.

Block-and-plinth casing

Block-and-plinth casing employs thick corner blocks, usually with carved relied patterns, at the corners of the door casing. Install blocks at the head casing joints and plinth blocks between the side casing and the floor. The blocks should be nailed on after the side casings are fastened in place and before installing the head casing. The bottom inside corners usually are installed so they align with the top corner reveal marks on the jamb. The head casing butts in between both corner blocks, so fit it in place with one corner block nailed and the other one loose. Choose corner blocks sized large enough to overhang the outside edges of the side casings by at least as much as they project past the faces of the casings.

If you plan to stain rather than paint the moldings, orient the corner blocks so the end grain runs vertically to hide as much of it as possible—it tends to stain darker than face grain.

Corner blocks are also used in window trim installations, but usually only at the top corners. In window trim, it's common for the overall length of the corner block and head casing assembly to equal the stool length.

How to Install Plinth Blocks

1 Plinth blocks should be parallel to the inside edge of the door jamb and they should follow the line of the floor. To accomplish both, position each block against the reveal line you've drawn on the edge of the jamb and rest the bottom of the block on the floor. If the block doesn't follow the floor exactly, use a compass and pencil to scribe a trimming line on the bottom of the block, following the floor contour.

2 Trim the plinth block along the scribed cutting line, checking to make sure the tops of both blocks are level with one another. Attach the blocks to the jambs with 8d finish nails—two nails in the jamb and two in the jack stud. The bottoms of the blocks should be resting flat on the floor (but do not attach the block to the floor). Set nailheads and use putty to conceal nail holes.

How to Install Corner Blocks

1 Install the side casings so they're aligned with the reveal lines on the side and top jambs. Position one of the corner blocks so the inside edge is flush with the side jamb. Nail it in place with 8d nails driven into the top jamb and the header.

2 Cut the head casing piece so it fits flush against the first corner block, is aligned with the top jamb reveal line, and extends just up to the inside edge of the other piece of side casing. Nail the second corner block in place, flush against the end of the head casing and the top of the side casing.

Baseboard & Wall Treatments

Baseboard is a transitional molding that could be classified as either a wall molding or a floor molding—although the distinction isn't really very important. But since it is attached to the wall, we decided to lump it together with other moldings that are attached to walls, including wainscotting, chair rail, picture rail and even fireplace mantels.

Like other molding types, baseboard and other wall treatments have multiple purposes that are both functional and decorative. Baseboard serves mostly to conceal the gaps between walls and floors, but it also protects the fragile bottom of the wall covering. And, especially when installing more elaborate, multi-piece basemolding, it can provide a strong decorative ele-

ment in the room. Wainscot is mostly a decorative wall treatment, but it's also a good way to conceal non-structural wall problems, and can be used to fur out a wall covering or provide additional space for running electrical cabling. Chair rail provides a strong horizontal line that can be a real visual boost to a dull room, and it also protects the wall surface from the backs of chairs that are leaned up against the wall—hence its name.

Picture rail and plate rail add elegance to just about any room, while providing an attractive and space-saving way to display your favorite art pieces and knick knacks.

Baseboard and base shoe molding work together to conceal gaps between the walls and floor, while adding an element of style and increasing the visual interest of a room.

Baseboard

Occasionally, homes are built without some kinds of trim, like casing around windows, decorative crown or picture rail. But you'd have to look long and far to find a home that has no baseboard. Baseboard has always served a useful function: it hides the gap formed where floors meet walls. There's no practical way to create a smooth, even seam between walls and floors, and depending on the type of flooring, a tight fit might actually create problems. In the case of solid wood flooring, for instance, the wood continually expands and contracts as humidity levels change, so the floor needs room for expansion—either beneath the wall surface or next to it— to allow for wood movement. Baseboard forms a slip joint over the floor, hiding the gap but allowing the wood to expand and contract. For uneven floors or

those with a definite texture, like stone or tile, baseboard can be scribed to follow irregular surfaces like the dips formed at grout lines. Regardless of the type of flooring, baseboard also protects the delicate bottom edges of walls from damage caused by foot traffic, furniture, vacuum cleaners and the like.

Aside from its function, baseboard also serves a decorative purpose. It creates a visual transition between walls and floors and helps tie the two surfaces together in a way that looks finished and intentional. Usually, baseboard matches the wood type, style and finish of the rest of the woodwork in a room, so it blends with its surroundings. Depending on the moldings you choose, however, baseboard can be as decorative and eye-catching as you like, adding a bit of elegance or charm.

Baseboard is one of the easier types of trim to install. Whether you choose simple case molding for your base, or a more elaborate scheme that includes several different kinds of molding in the design, the process for installing baseboard is the same. The only real difference is the time involved; you may have to make several laps around the room to add more moldings to the first course you nail in place. If you're embarking on

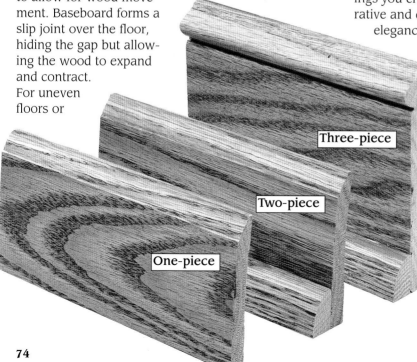

Three-piece

Two-piece

One-piece

Base trim (left) can be formed using just a single trim board, without base shoe or quarter-round molding (one-piece). Or, it can employ a trim board and base shoe (two-piece). Three-piece base molding has a cap rail attached on top of the base trim piece.

your first baseboard project, this chapter will outline the process for planning and installing base trim in any room. You'll also learn scribing and cutting techniques used by the pros for making tight-fitting joints. With this information under your belt, you should be able to trim out an average room with baseboard in less than a day's time. If you've installed baseboard in the past, use this chapter to refresh your memory of basic skills and techniques.

When to install baseboard. Baseboard is an example of *running trim* that is installed horizontally around the perimeter of a room. In new construction, baseboard is one of the last trim elements to be installed. It always overlays the interior wall sheathing, whether it be plaster, wallboard, sheet paneling or wainscot, so it should be attached after the walls are essentially finished. Do not install baseboard directly to wall framing. If you are installing baseboard over walls that still need to be painted, it's a good idea to paint the walls first all the way to the floor, then install the base. Otherwise, you'll have to mask off the molding later or use an edge guide when painting the walls to create a clean edge between the wall and the molding.

Baseboard butts against door casing, and it should either butt against or wrap around other obstructions, like heat registers. For this reason, hang door casing

and mount register plates before installing the base. If you need to create openings in the baseboard for electrical boxes, be sure to check your local building codes for guidelines on how to extend the boxes out to the surface of the molding. Most codes require that the front edges of electrical boxes not be recessed more than ¼ in. from the surrounding wall surface. It is also a code violation to conceal a "live" electrical box behind baseboard, so remove those boxes and disconnect any electrical wiring that no longer will be used once the baseboard is in place.

Generally, baseboard is installed after finished floors are laid, but this isn't a hard and fast rule. Solid-wood floors should not butt against baseboard, or the flooring could buckle when it expands. If you plan to add a new finished floor, check the manufacturer's recommendations for creating expansion gaps where the walls and floors meet. Depending on the manufacturer, you may be able to leave old baseboard in place and simply raise the base shoe (if your baseboard has it). But the foolproof solution is to simply lay the floor first, them install the baseboard over it. Carpeting can be laid after baseboard is up and simply butt against it. Vinyl flooring and other types of synthetic sheet flooring should tuck under baseboard to hide the cut edges, so install the flooring first.

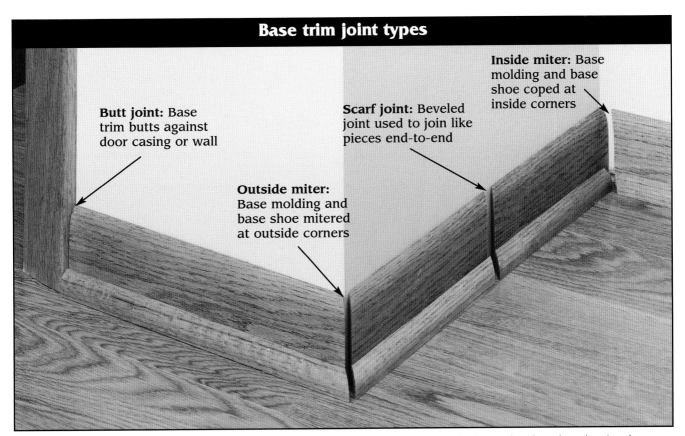

Base trim joint types

Butt joint: Base trim butts against door casing or wall

Outside miter: Base molding and base shoe mitered at outside corners

Scarf joint: Beveled joint used to join like pieces end-to-end

Inside miter: Base molding and base shoe coped at inside corners

Four primary joint types are all that are needed for just about any installation of base trim. Typically, the trim boards are butted against door casings and against one of the walls on an inside corner; the other joining trim at inside corners is coped to fit over the first piece (called a coped joint). Outside miters are made by beveling the trim pieces at mating 45° angles. Scarf joints are used to join trim pieces end-to-end in longer runs.

FLOORCOVERING DICTATES BASE TREATMENT

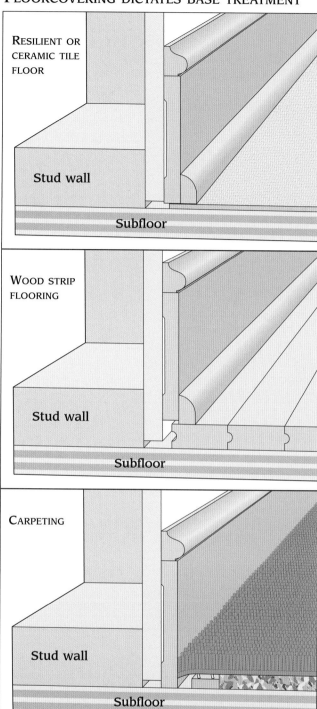

RESILIENT OR CERAMIC TILE FLOOR

Stud wall

Subfloor

WOOD STRIP FLOORING

Stud wall

Subfloor

CARPETING

Stud wall

Subfloor

Choose a base trim strategy that makes sense with your floorcovering. The type of floorcovering you have in place (or plan to install) affects both the type and timing of the base trim installation. If your floorcovering material is wood strip, tile or just about any other "hard" surface, you'll normally want to install the base trim (or at least the base shoe) after the installation of the floorcovering is complete. If the room will be carpeted, the easiest sequence for trimming the base of the wall is to install a base board (cap is optional), then install carpet tack strips, pad and carpeting. In most cases, base shoe is not used with carpeting, since the carpet material is butted up to and tucked against the base board, concealing the gap between the baseboard and the subfloor.

Baseboard design options. Aside from the specific molding profiles you choose for your baseboard, there is really only one other consideration: whether to use a *single-piece* or *multi-piece* treatment.

Single-piece baseboard can be as simple as a wide strip of base shoe or quarter-round molding, but more commonly it consists of a of flat base molding, usually with a profile milled along the top edge. Case molding for doors and windows can double as single-piece baseboard, especially if you plan to use the same molding around doors and windows. Numerous pre-milled base molding styles are also available in widths greater than standard case molding, so don't limit your search to only case molding. Premilled baseboard usually has a recess along the back face for fitting over irregular surfaces. Another option for making single-piece baseboard is to use dimensional lumber and rout a decorative profile along the top edge.

Installing single-piece baseboard is generally faster than installing multi-piece styles. If the molding is thin and made of a softwood like pine, it also will conform reasonably well to walls that aren't flat. Hardwood baseboard is much stiffer than softwood and will be more difficult to pull tight against wavy walls. You'll probably have to spend some time shaving down high spots on the wall first to make the wall conform to the molding. Otherwise, the next best option to hide gaps between the wall and the molding is to fill them with latex-based caulk or wallboard compound and sand these areas smooth.

For all floorcoverings except carpeting, you'll need to scribe and trim the bottom edge of the molding when using a single-piece treatment (See pages 86 to 87). Although this process isn't particularly difficult, it is somewhat time-consuming and finicky, but scribing is necessary in order to form reasonably tight joints between the floor and the baseboard.

Multi-piece baseboard (also called built-up baseboard) consists of two or three moldings stacked together to look like one piece. One option is to start with a course of basemolding, usually with a top profile, then build out the bottom edge of the molding with a strip of base shoe, quarter-round or narrow cove molding to hide gaps at the floor. For a more traditional look, start with a wide strip of basemolding or dimensional lumber with a flat top edge, then add a base cap along the top edge. Dress the bottom edge with base shoe, quarter-round or cove. This three-part design offers the most versatility in style.

There are several benefits to installing multi-piece baseboard. First, base cap and base shoe moldings, or their equivalent, are relatively thin and pliable so they're easy to nail against an undulating wall or floor to hide gaps. This way, there's no need to scribe the bottom edge of the wider basemolding. If you use base cap, it will function like base shoe to hide gaps formed between the basemolding and the wall.

Tips for installing baseboard.

Baseboard installation will go much easier if you take some time to "size up" the room and prepare your supplies beforehand. Here are some helpful tips to save time and spare your patience later.

• *Flatten wall surfaces, if possible.* Position a long level or a board with a flat edge against the wall in the baseboard area, working your way all around the room. Take note of where the walls dip and bow along their length. Some possible causes of these undulations are wall framing defects, especially where the studs meet the sole plate, or bulging caused by built-up wallboard compound. Flatten the high spots with a Surform plane or an old chisel. If you use a chisel, score the wallboard paper first with a utility knife to prevent tearing. Another way to flatten bulges is to drive a few wallboard screws into the bulge to pull the wallboard more tightly against the framing. Be sure to keep your repair efforts contained at least 1/4 in. below the height of the baseboard so they'll be covered once the base is installed.

• *Snap reference lines.* Baseboard is so far below our line of sight that it really doesn't matter if the moldings are perfectly level. Your frame of reference for baseboard is the floor, so as long as the height of the baseboard remains fairly consistent relative to the floor, it will look level. Still, it's a good practice to snap a chalkline around the room to mark the baseboard height. Use this reference line as a guide for lining up the top edges of the moldings when you install them. Unless you plan to scribe and trim the bottom edges of the baseboard, as with single-piece baseboard schemes, you'll want to establish the chalkline at the highest point of the floor. This way, the gap formed beneath the baseboard in the lowest area of the floor can be concealed with the shoe molding. Be sure the distance from the floor to the chalk line isn't greater than the combined width of the baseboard and shoe molding.

• *Cut the moldings to rough length.* One way to be sure you've got enough molding to complete a baseboard job is cut the strips to rough length first, then lay them next to their corresponding positions on the wall. This way, you'll commit the longer strips of baseboard where they're needed most, allowing you to plan out your cuts on the rest of the molding pieces to minimize waste. Leave each length of molding at least 2 in. longer than necessary so you'll have ample extra material for cutting and fitting the end joints.

TIPS FOR INSTALLING BASEBOARD

Apply the finish first. Whether priming and painting or staining and varnishing, if you pre-finish the workpieces then all that's left to do is touch up holes left by the nailheads. It isn't even necessary to pre-cut the molding to length first; simply finish to the molding pieces while they're still full-length. If you are installing wood moldings, it's a good practice to apply finish to both the front and back faces so the wood will absorb moisture more evenly and not warp. For synthetic moldings that aren't sensitive to moisture, just finish the front face.

Mark wall stud locations. You'll nail baseboard to the wall at both the sole plate and the wall studs. Nailing will go much faster and be more accurate if you mark the stud locations first, outside the area that will be covered by the baseboard. Use an electronic stud finder to locate the first couple of studs. Once you know the span between the studs—usually 16 in. on-center—you can step off the rest of the studs with a tape measure, marking stud locations every 16 in. TIP: Use strips of masking tape to the wall, then mark the center of the stud on each piece of tape.

Draw an installation diagram

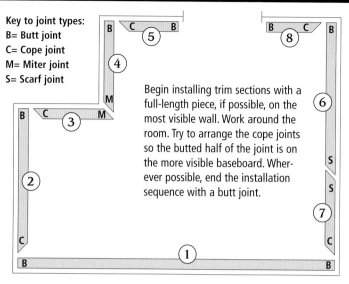

Key to joint types:
B= Butt joint
C= Cope joint
M= Miter joint
S= Scarf joint

Begin installing trim sections with a full-length piece, if possible, on the most visible wall. Work around the room. Try to arrange the cope joints so the butted half of the joint is on the more visible baseboard. Wherever possible, end the installation sequence with a butt joint.

Draw a birdseye sketch of the room that includes all wall surfaces that will be fitted with baseboard. Include the closet if you plan to run the baseboard there as well. Mark doorways or other obstructions, like protruding heat registers, that will break the baseboard run. Then draw a set of reference lines to indicate the baseboard. The purpose of this sketch is to identify what joints you'll use to connect each piece of baseboard together and how the two parts of each joint relate to one another. For butt and cope joints, show which half of the joint butts against the wall and which piece of baseboard overlaps the other. Draw the miter joints for outside corners as well. Finally, mark any baseboard strips that will need to be made with more than one continuous piece of molding, and show the orientation of the scarf joint you'll need to make to join the sections together. Once you make these determinations, label the order in which you'll install the molding pieces, from first to last. This exercise might seem a little excessive, but the floorplan will keep you from forgetting your overall installation approach and help you recall how the joint parts fit together, so you won't mistakenly miscut the parts.

Back-beveling cuts

If you're installing baseboard with a top profile, set your miter saw about 5° off of square, and back-cut both ends of the baseboard with the molding standing upright against the saw fence. This technique, called *back-beveling*, allows just the front edges of the butt joints to make full contact with the adjacent wall surfaces. The slight gaps formed along the back edges of these ends will be hidden by the coped ends of the adjacent baseboards.

5° back-bevel

Choosing baseboard joints (See photo, page 75).

Rooms present three different wall situations that determine baseboard joint selection. In the first, baseboard fits between two walls, and both ends of the molding fit into inside wall corners. A second scenario is where a wall forms an inside corner on one end but makes an outside corner on the other end. A third circumstance, found at the ends of knee walls or open entryways without doors, is a wall with two outside corners. Here are the basic joint options:

Inside corner joints. Where baseboard meets at an inside corner, the best joint to use for moldings with a top profile is a cope joint (See page 81). You may be tempted to make a miter joint instead, but copes fit more tightly and are more forgiving than miters. And if a cope joint opens up as the moldings shrink, the gap will be less noticeable than a miter joint. If you are installing flat baseboard with no top profile, the most sensible and quickest joints to use are butt joints. In fact, on multi-piece baseboards with base cap, most of the top edge of these butt joints will be concealed by the cap molding. Still, it is important that the inside corner formed where the butted pieces meet is as tight-fitting as possible. Use the scribing techniques on pages 86 to 87 to mark and cut these butt joints so they'll fit tightly.

Outside corner joints. Whether you are fitting flat-edged or profiled baseboard, miter joints are the only way to hide the molding's end grain and continue the profile around a corner without breaking the profile shape. The trouble with miter joints and baseboard is that walls often are not plumb and outside corners aren't always square. Follow the procedures on pages 82 to 84 for cutting outside miters and double miters.

Scarf joints. These are essentially splice joints used to join sections of trim end-to-end in longer runs. See page 88.

General strategies for installing baseboard.

There's a logic to installing baseboard in an orderly fashion, and it has to do with how the joints fit together. The sequence you follow for installing the baseboard strips establishes the orientation of the joints. It also influences which joints will benefit from the extra waste material factored into the length of the pieces. Since miter joints are particularly fussy to fit together, you'll want to make the easier joints first and leave the extra length for fitting the miter joints.

Here are some general guidelines to help you plan a strategy for installing baseboard.

• *Make a floorplan* (See Tip box, previous page). Label the drawing to show the order you'll install the pieces.

• *Choose a smart sequence.* The first piece of baseboard you install should be on the wall opposite the entry door. Generally, this is the longest and most visible wall in the room. Mark this piece of baseboard so it butts all the way into both wall corners. This way, both ends will be covered by adjoining pieces of baseboard.

Lay out the rest of the inside corner joints in the room with either butt joints for flat-edged baseboard or cope joints for baseboard with a profiled top edge. Try to arrange the cope joints so the butted half of the joint is on the more visible baseboard. Keep the coped pieces arranged so they are at right angles to your line of sight. Avoid laying out a strip of baseboard that requires a cope joint on each end. Such pieces will be difficult to cut and fit tightly.

• *End the installation with a butt joint.* However you arrange your installation sequence for installing the base, try to make the last piece you install be one with a cope joint on one end and a butt joint on the other. Fit the coped end first, then mark, cut and fit the butted end.

How to Install Baseboard

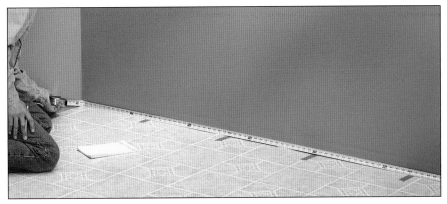

1 The first piece of baseboard you'll install on the wall opposite the entry door has square butt joints on both ends. To fit this piece, first measure the overall length of the wall from corner to corner. Be sure to measure near the floor in the baseboard area, since the adjacent walls may not be plumb. Add 1/16 in. to this measurement, and cut the strip of baseboard to this length. Make cuts using a back-beveling technique (See Tip box, previous page).

2 Set the first piece of base in position so the ends fit tightly into the wall corners and the top edge aligns with your chalk reference line (if you drew one). Since the molding is cut slightly long, it should bow out gradually at the center. Press the molding against the wall until it snaps into place and lays flat. Doing so will also force the ends of the molding to dig into the walls slightly for a tight fit. If the baseboard continues to bow when you try to press it flat, trim a little off one end to shorten the workpiece, and it should snap flat.

3 Nail the baseboard to the wall with a pair of 6d or 8d nails at each stud location. Drive one nail into the wall's sole plate and the other into the wall stud, angling the nails slightly downward so they help pull the baseboard tighter to the wall. If your baseboard scheme includes shoe moldings along the floor, drive the bottom nails close enough to the floor so the heads will be concealed by the shoe. Nail from one end of the molding to the other, keeping the top edge aligned with your chalkline.

(Continued next page)

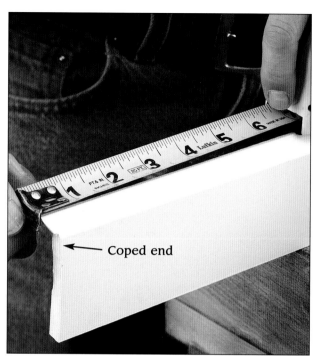

Coped end

4 Other baseboard pieces (besides the first) in your floorplan will need to fit between pairs of walls as well. Likely as not, the second piece you install will be this type. If your baseboard has a molded top profile, the end of the second piece that fits over the end of the first piece will need to be coped (See next page). The other end of this second piece of molding should receive a square butt joint to set up the next cope joint. To fit the second, and subsequent lengths of base with both coped and butted ends, always cut the coped end to shape first. Once you've cut the cope, press the coped end against the first piece of baseboard to check the fit of the joint. Improve the fit, if necessary, by shaping the coped end further with a file.

5 Measure between the walls and mark the length of the base-board from the top corner of the coped end, adding 1/16 in. to the overall length for a snap fit.

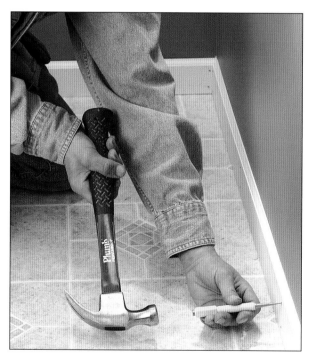

6 Cross-cut the molding to length. Press the ends of the mold-ing into place, snap the molding flush to the wall, and nail as you did the first baseboard piece. Continue working around the room, installing a butt joint last if possible.

TIP: CLOSING GAPS. Depending on how wavy your walls are, you may still end up with gaps between the molding and the wall in the bay areas between the wall studs where there's nothing to nail to. One solution is to drive a 16d finish nail down at a sharp angle near the top of the molding where it gaps, so the nail hits the sole plate. Unless your moldings are par-ticularly wide, this trick should pull the molding tight.

1 Cut one strip of baseboard for the joint so the end runs all the way into the corner formed by the two walls. This is the butted half of the cope joint. Nail the butted baseboard to the wall. Cut the other piece of baseboard for the inside corner so the overall length of this molding strip is a few inches longer than needed for the wall. The end of this baseboard will form the coped edge that fits over the butted piece. Begin to form the coped end of the baseboard by miter-cutting the end to 45°. Set the saw so that the toe of the miter points toward the back face of the molding, just as you would cut the piece if you were using miter joints instead. The miter cut exposes the molding's profile in cross-section and provides a reference line for cutting the cope. This inside edge will fit against the face of the butted piece once the molding is coped to shape.

2 Highlight the inside edge of the miter so it's easier to see by rubbing along the edge of the profile with a pencil.

3 Clamp the molding to a worksurface and saw along the profile with a coping saw to remove the waste created by the miter. You can orient the blade on the saw with the teeth facing forward so it cuts on the push stroke, or flip the blade so the teeth face the handle and cut on the pull stroke. If you prefer to cut on the pull stroke, position yourself so the saw handle is below the molding and work the saw up and down from below. Either way, start the cut so the saw is nearly perpendicular to the molding, then angle the saw as you make the cut toward the back of the molding at about 60° to 80°, forming a back bevel. The back bevel will allow just the coped edge to fit against the butted piece of base. Cut on the waste side of the profile edge. You may need to cut out the waste in several smaller pieces and change the angle of the back bevel, depending on the profile.

4 Test-fit the coped piece of base against the butted piece to see how the joint fits. Then, refine the coped edge as needed by filing away more material from the back bevel using a rat-tail or half-round file. Sandpaper wrapped around a pencil also works. Work carefully in the area that forms a point at the top end of the coped edge to keep from breaking it. Support the point with your index finger held against the top edge of the molding while you file or sand it.

Cutting outside miters

Fitting baseboard at outside corners would be easy if walls always met at 90° angles. But more often than not, they don't. Miter joints are the best way to wrap base around outside corners, and it's important that the joints fit tightly. The trouble is, you can't be sure that each half of the miter joint forms a 45° angle. One way to determine the saw angle setting is to wrap a bevel gauge around the outside corner, lock the gauge to the angle and check it against a protractor to measure the angle. Divide this angle by two to determine the angle of each of the miters in the joint.

If you don't have a protractor handy, another approach is to draw layout lines on the floor and bisect the outside corner angle. Once you've bisected the corner angle, you can use the layout lines to both set the saw and mark the moldings themselves for making accurate miter cuts.

2 Draw a line that extends from the wall corner out through the baseboard corner you found in Step 1, and a few inches beyond. This is the bisect line for the corner joint. Set a bevel gauge so it matches the angle formed by one of the two layout lines in Step 1 and the bisecting line of Step 2. Use the bevel gauge to set the miter saw angle for cutting the baseboard.

HOW TO MAKE OUTSIDE MITER JOINTS IN BASEBOARD

1 Take a scrap of baseboard and, holding it against one wall so it extends past the corner, draw a line along the front edge of the molding on the floor. Repeat the process with the molding held against the adjacent wall of the corner. The point where the two lines meet on the floor marks the outside corner of the baseboard.

3 Position the baseboard piece for one side of the corner joint against the wall and mark where the workpiece crosses the wall corner, as well as where it intersects the point you found in Step 1. Repeat this process on the baseboard strip that will cover the other side of the corner. Both of these strips of baseboard should have a few inches of waste material that extend beyond the marks you've just made.

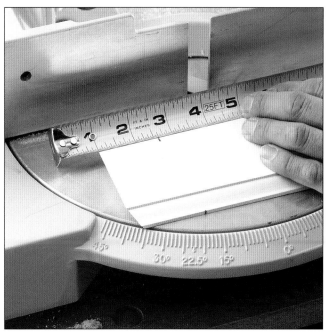

4 Use the bevel gauge to transfer the cutting angle to your miter saw. Trim the workpiece to rough length by cutting it 2 in. past the reference marks, on the waste side. Cut both boards to rough length.

5 Measure back from the cut edge to each of the reference marks on the board. If the distances match, it means that the wall is plumb. If the distances do not match, you'll need to shim beneath the molding to raise or lower one edge of the board—See next step.

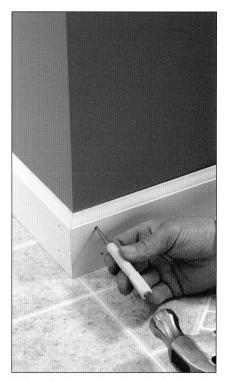

6 For walls that are out of plumb, slip a shim beneath the baseboard on the saw table to change the cutting angle of the blade in relation to the molding. How much you'll need to change the angle involves some trial and error. Slide the shim closer to the blade if the bottom edge of the molding is too long. Slide the molding away from the blade to shorten the top edge. Make additional test cuts, sliding the shim closer or further from the blade until the distances from the reference marks on the molding to the test-cut edge are equal. Hold the shim in this position, realign the molding and cut to your reference marks.

7 Test-fit the baseboard against both walls. Trim the mitered edges with a low-angle block plane as needed until the corner joint closes without leaving a gap. Nail the baseboard sections in place. Set the nailheads with a nailset.

Cutting double miters

Cutting and fitting a length of baseboard with miter joints on both ends (a double miter) is simply a matter of building the miter joint for a single outside corner, then doing it again on the other end of the board. The most likely times you'll run into this situation are when working with knee walls, open doorways (no door and jambs) or on bump-outs where walls conceal obstructions, such as a chimney chase. Begin by cutting and fitting the boards to make the first miter joint (See pages 82 to 83). But do not cut the second board (the one that needs miters on both ends) to its finished length yet.

HOW TO CUT BASEBOARD WITH AN OUTSIDE MITER AT EACH END

1 Cut and fit the miter on one end of the molding first (See pages 82 to 83), letting the other end of the molding run past the opposite outside corner. Once you've got a tight-fitting miter joint for the first outside corner, mark and cut the long end of the molding to form the first half of the second outside miter joint.

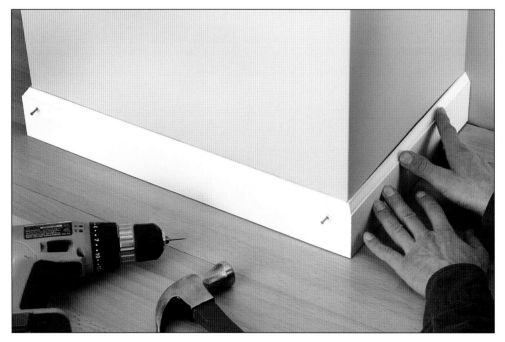

2 Tack this piece of base in place, and proceed with making the baseboard strip that will complete the second miter joint, cutting and fitting the inside corner joint first (either a cope or butt joint), then cutting and fitting the outside miter. Working your way around the outside corners in sequence is an easier approach than trying to cut and fit both mitered ends of the baseboard at once, then fitting this piece between the two other baseboards with mitered ends. Once the boards are cut and fit, nail them in permanently.

Working around obstructions

As you work your way around the room, eventually you'll need to terminate the baseboard where it meets door casings. The common convention for treating base in these situations is to butt the base against the casing. Usually the baseboard will be thinner than the casing, so the base and casing will form a pleasing reveal.

For other obstructions, like heat registers, that stand proud of the wall, butt the base molding portion of the baseboard against the sides of the register. Use a preacher (See Tip, right) held against the sides of the register to mark the cuts. If your baseboard includes base cap, run the base cap around the register, using miter joints at the upper corners. Another option, if your basemolding has a top profile instead, is to rip off the profiled portion on the table saw and wrap this profile around the register like base cap.

Making & using a preacher

There's no guarantee that the door casing is square to the baseboard, and since the baseboard/casing joint will be visible, you'll want a tight joint here. One solution is to cut the baseboard a little long, then shave the base down as needed for a snug fit against the casing. A faster method is to use a simple jig that trim carpenters call a "preacher." To make one, cut a notch a little wider and taller than the baseboard into a scrap of plywood, and inset the notch on the scrap a distance equal to the thickness of the baseboard. To use the preacher, slip the notch over the baseboard and slide it up tight to the back edge of the door casing. The preacher transfers the exact angle of the casing around to the front of the baseboard and provides a convenient straightedge for marking the angle onto the baseboard. Draw the cutting line on the baseboard and cut it to length. The baseboard should fit against the casing without leaving a gap.

WORKING AROUND A HEAT REGISTER

OPTION 1: The easiest way to deal with in-line obstructions, like a heat register grate, is simply to treat it like door casing and butt the basemolding against both edges.

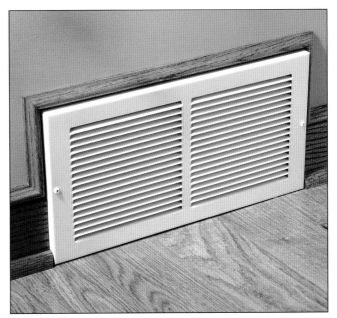

OPTION 2: For a more finished appearance, run cap molding around the top of the register grate, mitering all corners. This is easiest if using separate base cap molding, but you can do it with any style by rip-cutting a profiled section off the basemolding stock.

Scribing to follow a floor surface

Most floors aren't dead flat, especially in older homes. Floor framing sags some over time, and so does the flooring it supports. If you don't plan to install shoe moldings to hide gaps, you'll need to account for unevenness in the floor by scribing the base molding to follow the floor surface. Scribing simply involves transferring the floor's irregularities to the baseboard by tracing along the baseboard with a compass. Once you draw the floor's pattern along the base, trim the base to the line so the bottom edge of the molding can conform to the shape of the floor.

Before you decide to scribe your baseboard, give some serious consideration to a couple of factors:

• Once you scribe one baseboard, you're pretty much committed to scribing all of them. Reducing the height of one piece naturally means you'll have to trim the other so they all are level at the joints.

• If the trimming is not done neatly or the floor is extremely wavy, scribing can accentuate the unevenness of the floor, rather than disguise it.

For these reasons, installing base shoe is a much more popular solution, especially on houses with uneven floors. And installing base shoe will likely be faster than scribing and cutting the baseboard. But if you're looking to create a contemporary trim appearance, one-piece baseboard is still your best bet.

HOW TO SCRIBE & TRIM BASEBOARD

1 Use a long level held against a straight board to find the lowest spot in the floor. Cut each piece of baseboard to length, making miter or cope cuts at the ends as necessary. Begin with the piece of baseboard that will be attached to the wall closest to the low area. Level the top edge of the baseboard, then tack it to the wall with a few finish nails to hold it in place while you scribe the molding to the floor (drive the nails part way only so you can remove them without out damaging the molding). Set a compass so the distance between the points of the legs equals the widest gap formed where the bottom edge of the baseboard meets the floor. Orient the compass so the metal point touches the floor and the pencil point touches the molding. Drag the compass along the floor to draw a line along the baseboard. Be sure to keep the metal point and the pencil aligned up and down as you draw the scribe line. If either the metal point or the pencil get ahead of the other, the scribe line will be inaccurate.

2 Secure the first piece of baseboard to a sturdy worksurface then trim away the bottom edge of the base molding up to the scribe line. Use a jig saw with a fine wood-cutting blade, a block plane or a belt sander to form the scribed edge. If using a saw, lightly sand the bottom edge when you're done cutting to clean up the edge.

3 Set the baseboard in place and check the fit of the scribe, adjusting it as needed by trimming away more material. Once the fit is satisfactory, nail the molding in place. Repeat this process for the other molding strips around the room. You'll probably have to scribe some amount off of all the baseboards so the top edges align with one another.

Installing baseboard with a pneumatic nail gun

Installing baseboard is one trim carpentry task where pneumatic nail guns really earn their keep. If your accuracy with a hammer is less than perfect, it will get worse after you spend a few hours on your hands and knees nailing baseboard within inches of the floor. To make matters worse, nailing baseboard into corners will challenge your contortionist skills, as you bend and twist to gain the best advantage on the nail without banging walls, floors or fingers. A better solution all around is to rent, borrow or buy a pneumatic nail gun. Instead of the hit and miss process of swinging a hammer, you simply depress the nosepiece of the nailer where you want to put the nail and squeeze the trigger. Nail guns will both drive and set the nail in one action, and most are designed to fit into even the tightest corners.

Pneumatic nails are less likely to split wood than hand-driven finish nails, and you can buy them in a range of lengths. Select a nail size for your project that's long enough to penetrate the molding and wallboard, and extend into the framing about 3/4 in. A good general choice is a 16-gauge, 2-in. nail. To drive nails of this type and length, you'll need a finish nailer. To keep from overdriving the nails in either hard or softwood moldings, set the air compressor to about 90 psi. Test a few nails in the molding and adjust the air pressure up or down until the nailheads set about 1/16 in. below the molding surface.

Moldings with a cope cut at each end should be cut into two separate pieces that are joined with a scarf joint. This allows you to fit the more complicated cope cuts precisely. Bevel-cut the ends to form the scarf joint after the copes are cut.

Scarf joints in baseboard

To make the most efficient use of base moldings, you'll likely need to create longer pieces from two shorter strips. You could simply butt the ends of the strips together, but the faces of the moldings will be difficult to keep aligned this way when you nail them to the wall. A better way to mate the ends of the baseboard moldings (as with most molding types) is with a scarf joint.

Essentially, the joint is made by miter-cutting the ends of the moldings at opposite 45° angles so one mitered end overlaps the other. Scarf joints are also a good way to build a strip of baseboard that must have cope joints cut on both ends. By making a double-coped baseboard in two parts rather than as one continuous strip, you can cut the coped ends first and tweak them independently until each fits tightly into its joint. The scarf joint establishes the overall length of the molding when the two shorter strips are combined.

When laying out and fitting a scarf joint, try to locate it over a wall stud so you'll have adequate backing for nailing each half of the joint securely.

Cut and install baseboard that makes up the back half of the scarf joint first; this way, the other piece can be cut and trimmed for a nearly invisible seam with the first piece. Nail each half of the joint to the wall stud and sole plate with a pair of finish nails. Drive the nails for the overlap piece so they cross the scarf joint, locking it tightly together.

Closing a scarf joint in baseboard

Scarf joints create a nearly invisible seam when used to join two pieces of baseboard end to end. You'll get the best results if you locate the scarf joint over a wall stud. Attach the overlapped board first by driving a finish nail near the top and another near the bottom. Then, cut the overlapping piece and adjust the fit as needed until the boards meet perfectly. Drive two more nails through the overlapping joint at an angle so they catch the end of the first board and still hit the stud and sole plate. Pilot holes are recommended.

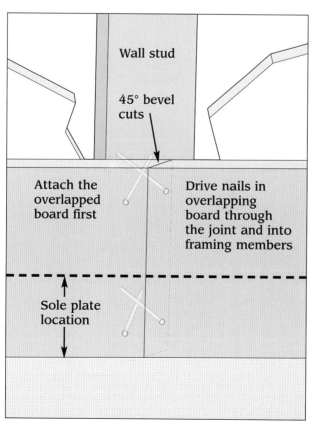

Wall stud

45° bevel cuts

Attach the overlapped board first

Drive nails in overlapping board through the joint and into framing members

Sole plate location

Base shoe & cap

Once the basemolding is installed around the room, you may want to add base shoe where the basemolding meets the floor, and perhaps base cap to cover the top edge. Base shoe and base cap are much narrower than basemolding, so it's acceptable to join the pieces at both inside and outside corners with miters if you like. For paint-grade work, you can hide small gaps at these miter joints with latex caulk, then touch up with primer and paint. If the baseboard has a clear finish, however, a better solution is to cut cope joints, not miters, for the inside corners. Work your way around the room in the same manner as you installed the basemolding.

The nailing process differs for base shoe and base cap. Drive nails for the shoe moldings down at an angle and into the floor, rather than straight into the basemolding. This way, if the basemolding shrinks across its width or the floor settles over time, the base shoe will remain tight to the floor, hiding any gaps that form at the floor.

Trim carpenters differ in opinion when it comes to nailing base cap. In order for these cap moldings to hug wall surfaces tightly, it makes sense to nail them to wall studs rather than down into the top edge of the basemolding. If you do it this way, the base cap will stay put even if the basemolding shrinks widthwise, which could open up a gap between the cap and the top of the basemolding. But if you nail the cap to the basemolding instead, it may limit how well you can make the cap fit tightly to the wall. You'll have to choose which shortcoming is more forgivable.

Shoe moldings usually project beyond the door casing after they're attached. Where this is the case, bevel-cut the end of the shoe molding away from the casing at a 45° angle so it appears to taper toward the casing. Use this same approach for other cases where the shoe moldings stop—such as where the shoe meets a heat register that stands out from the wall.

Install cap molding first, using miter joints at both inside and outside corners (you may prefer to cope inside corners, but it's generally felt that the payback is not worth the effort). Base shoe, however, is often coped at inside corners because it is subject to more stresses and the miter joints are more likely to open.

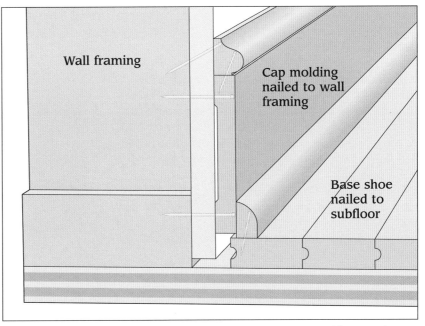

Wall framing

Cap molding nailed to wall framing

Base shoe nailed to subfloor

Nailing base shoe and cap. Base shoe should always be nailed to the subfloor, not the basemolding so it can move with the floor, preventing the formation of gaps. Cap molding is generally nailed to wall framing members, but many carpenters prefer to attach it to the top of the basemolding. You may choose either method—just don't do both.

Chair rail generally is made with running moldings and often includes a cap molding top. It is installed between 32 and 36 inches above the floor, where it protects wall surfaces from the backs of chairs. It can be attached to the wall by nailing at each wall stud location, although installing backer (See page 98) will allow a sturdier, tighter installation. Typically, outside corners are mitered and inside corners are coped.

Chair, Picture & Shelf Rail

In addition to baseboard, there are a few more wall moldings you may want to consider adding to a room. Among the more common are *chair rail, picture rail and shelf rail* (sometimes called *plate rail* or *plate shelf*). All three are classified as running moldings, so they install horizontally around the room, just like baseboard. But unlike baseboard, chair, picture and shelf rail often are installed on only one or two walls in the room. Chair, picture and shelf rail can provide an attractive trim detail to any room, but you'll usually see them reserved for rooms that serve more formal, elegant purposes, such as dining and living rooms.

Chair rail. Chair rail, which may consist of a simple flat molding or a flat molding capped with a wider molding, typically is mounted between 32 and 36 in. above the floor. It does what it's name implies: it protects walls from dings and scuffs caused by chair backs. Chair rail is a good way to cap wainscot or beadboard paneling because it covers the top edges of the boards. Visually, it also makes an interesting wall

Shelf rail option

Use hardwood spindles to create a railing for your shelf rail assembly. The spindles (⅝ dia. × 1¼ in. long oak spindles are shown here) can be found at woodworking stores and craft stores. Simply drill guide holes for the spindles in the base piece and the railing, then glue them into the holes (right photo). You'll still need to cut a groove in the base piece to support the plates.

Picture rail is installed near the joint where the walls meet the ceiling. There must be enough free space above the top of the molding to fit a picture hook over the cylindrical edge of the molding. Its appearance is similar to a smaller sprung molding installed as a crown molding.

How to hang picture rail & chair rail

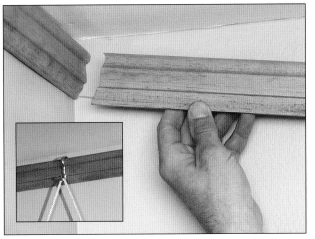

1 The techniques for installing picture rail and chair rail are virtually identical, except that picture rail is attached 7 to 8 feet above the floor, and chair rail is fastened 32 to 36 in. above the floor. Start by snapping a level reference line all around the room. For picture molding, make sure the reference line represents the bottom edge of the molding.

2 Make cope cuts to create inside corner joints (See page 81). Outside corner joints can be mitered (See pages 82 to 83). Drive finish nails at wall stud locations and, if possible, up and into the wall cap plate. If you plan to hang framed art from the rail and can't get fasteners into the cap plate, install backer boards (See page 98). Slip picture rail hooks (inset photo) over the cylinder on the top edge.

divider. You can enhance the effect by painting the area below the chair rail a darker color than the wall area above the molding, or by painting one area (usually the upper section) and wallpapering the other.

Picture rail. Picture rail, which mounts between 7 and 8 ft. above the floor, is a one-piece molding with a cylindrical projection that runs along its top edge. Picture rail molding is sold in a number of widths and shapes, but all have the uniform top cylinder. The cylinder part is designed to hold specialized metal hooks that support pictures (you can buy picture rail hooks at hardware stores and framing shops). For rooms with 8-ft. ceilings, picture rail can function as a cornice, perhaps combined with crown molding for a more elaborate ceiling treatment.

Cornice-style shelf rail

This "cornice-style" shelf rail is built using stock crown molding and MDF ripped and shaped to size for the back board and shelf. The dimensions indicated on the drawing below can be used as a guide for building the shelf rail as it is shown here. You may want to alter the dimensions based on the size of your room and the actual size of the crown molding you choose. Build as much of the assembly as you can on your shop table, then install it. It's best to leave the crown molding off until after the backer/shelf assembly is fastened to the wall—you'll get a more solid connection and the crown molding can then conceal the screws driven through the backer board and into the wall studs. As long as you have access to drive a couple of good sturdy screws at each wall stud location, it shouldn't be necessary to reinforce with additional backer boards between the wall studs in the wall cavity. See pages 93 to 94.

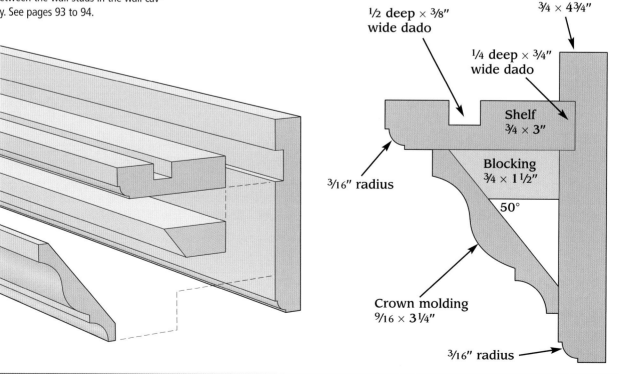

Back board
3/4 × 4 3/4"

1/2 deep × 3/8" wide dado

1/4 deep × 3/4" wide dado

Shelf
3/4 × 3"

3/16" radius

Blocking
3/4 × 1 1/2"

50°

Crown molding
9/16 × 3 1/4"

3/16" radius

Shelf rail (plate shelf). Shelf rail is generally installed either at eye level or 16-to-24 in. down from the ceiling. Almost always made from multiple pieces, it has a running groove or a small railing in front to support plates. The railing can be solid or, in more elaborate treatments, it may be a spindle-and-rail style. You can purchase premilled moldings to create shelf rail, or you can make them yourself by milling stock lumber goods. The two plans shown in this section represent two very different approaches to designing self rail. The cornice-style molding has a very traditional, cabinet-type appearance and uses stick crown molding for the front. With structural members made from MDF, it is designed to be painted. The contemporary shelf rail plan has a softer appearance and is made from hardwood so it can be clear-coated.

While chair rails, picture rail and shelf rail each can contribute significantly to the appearance of a room, the effectiveness tends to be diminished if you install two or more types of wall moldings.

Installation tips. Because most wall moldings should be installed with sturdy backers attached to or between the wall studs, the easiest time to install them is before the wallcovering is attached. That way, you can plan for the installation by attaching backing or bridging into the wall cavity (See page 98). When installing chair rail, you can probably get by fastening into wall studs only—there is relatively little stress on chair rail. But picture rail and shelf rail should always be fastened to sturdy backing—even if it means you have to retrofit the backing behind the existing wall surface (See page 98). The best backing is 2 × 4 blocking installed between the wall studs, or a continuous strip of 1 × 4 notched into the studs before the wallboard goes up.

Once you've solved the problem of having adequate backing, the

HOW TO MAKE & INSTALL CORNICE-STYLE SHELF RAIL

1 Draw a diagram of your installation plan so you can correctly calculate the required lengths of the shelf rail sections. Rip the stock for the back boards and the shelf parts to width (we used MDF). Cut the profiles and dadoes into the full length sections. Use a router (a router table is better) and a 3/16 in. bead bit to shape the lower edge profiles. We used a dado-blade set mounted in the table saw to cut the dadoes in the shelves and back boards.

2 Cut the back board and shelf for each section. Cut them each a few inches longer than the required length. Bevel-rip blocking to fit at the underside of each shelf/back board joint. Glue and nail the back boards, shelves and blocking together to form the assemblies. Do not attach the crown molding yet. Apply your finish of choice to the assemblies.

(Continued next page)

3 Snap level chalklines all around the room. Carefully measure the length of each section and trim the appropriate section of shelf rail to fit. Miter the ends of the assemblies. Make each assembly slightly longer than your final measurement, test the fit, then trim bit by bit until the fit is perfect. Attach to the wall at stud locations. We used #8 × 3½ in. wood screws at each wall stud. Do not attach the ends until both sections making the inside corner are tacked in place. Close the miters as best you can, then screw the ends to the corner wall studs.

4 Cut the crown molding to fit and install beneath the shelf on each section. Normally, sprung moldings are coped at inside corners, but because of the structure of the shelf rail you'll need to create miter joints instead. Use a jig to make accurate miter cuts in the crown molding (See page 139). Fill nail holes in crown molding with tinted wood putty.

installation process for wall moldings is relatively easy. Mark a level line all around the room, and align the bottom edge of the molding to the line. Follow the same floorplan rules as you'd use for hanging cornice or baseboard: Start by installing molding on the wall opposite the main entryway and work your way around the room clockwise or counterclockwise. For picture rail and single-piece chair rail, use cope joints for joining the moldings at inside corners and miter joints for outside corners. If you are installing a multiple-piece molding and the cap molding is perpendicular to the flat molding beneath it, miter-cut the cap molding at inside corners. Use a scarf joint for building a longer strip of molding from two shorter strips, and try to position the scarf joint so it won't be conspicuous when you enter the room.

In most cases, picture rail won't meet window or door casing because it will be mounted above these openings. But you will have to fit both chair rail and shelf rail against window and door casing. If the molding is thinner than the casing, butt it up flush against the casing. If the molding is thick enough to project beyond the face of the casing, terminate the chair rail or shelf rail with a return miter. Or, notch the end of the molding so it fits around the casing and overlaps it. The length of the overlap should equal the amount the molding projects past the casing.

To fasten wall moldings to the wall and backer, use 6d or 8d finish nails for chair rail and picture rail that won't serve a structural purpose. Screws are a better choice for picture rail that will hold pictures, as well as for shelf rail—countersunk 2-in. wallboard or trimhead screws driven into pilot holes work well. Cover the screwheads with wood plugs, tinted wood putty or spackle.

Contemporary Shelf Rail

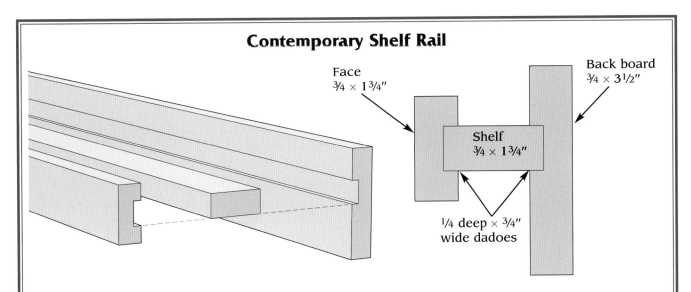

Face
¾ × 1¾"

Back board
¾ × 3½"

Shelf
¾ × 1¾"

¼ deep × ¾"
wide dadoes

HOW TO MAKE & INSTALL CONTEMPORARY SHELF RAIL

1 Draw a diagram of your installation plan so you can correctly calculate the required lengths of the shelf rail sections. Rip the stock for the back boards, faces and shelves. Cut ¼ deep × ¾ in. wide dadoes in each face and back board to accept a shelf. Glue and nail the shelf sections between the faces and back boards. The ends of all parts should be flush. Apply your finish of choice. Take exact measurements for each section and cut the assemblies slightly overlong. If the shelf rail will be installed on more than one wall, you'll need to make miter cuts at the ends. Test the fits and trim the sections to finished length.

2 Using a level chalkline as a reference, position the sections on the wall. At wall stud locations, drill a counterbored pilot hole for a #8 × 3½ in. screw (drive screws above the shelf so they are less visible). Fasten the shelf rail sections to the walls, checking for level as you work. Leave the ends free until all sections are installed so you can close the joints together before driving the final screws. Fill counterbore holes with wood plugs or tinted wood putty.

Custom-built, solid wood panels are time consuming and a bit tricky to make, but nothing can compare to them for richness, durability and uniqueness of appearance. Pages 106 to 115.

Tongue-and-groove boards give a room a rustic Country appearance that's very popular today. They're relatively cheap and easy to install yourself. Pages 100 to 105.

Wainscot

Before plaster became a common wall covering, interior walls in homes were often sheathed with wood boards called wainscot or wainscotting. Wood was the plentiful, easy solution for dividing up living spaces. Europeans began sheathing walls with wainscot during the Middle Ages, and the first American settlers from Europe brought this building practice with them. Take a tour of virtually any preserved home that was built in this country during the late 18th and 19th centuries, and you'll find at least one room trimmed with wainscot. Wainscot was common ornamentation for walls of parlors and common living areas, but it was also used in hallways, studies, kitchens and even bedrooms.

Following the industrial revolution, the rise of modern building materials and the increasing scarcity of lumber made wood a more expensive alternative for covering walls than plaster or eventually wallboard. Architectural design trends changed as a result, and solid wood was used more sparingly as a wall covering. Wainscot evolved from a floor-to-ceiling wall treatment to the partial wall covering we know today. Typically, wainscot extends from the floor to a height of 30 to 40 in. Floor-to-ceiling wood wall coverings generally are called paneling these days, not wainscot.

Despite the influence of newer and cheaper building materials and the ever-rising cost of lumber, wainscot has never completely been abandoned as a wall treatment. In fact, wainscot is making a comeback in homes today, along with more elaborate trim treatments like cornices, blocked window and door casings and multi-piece baseboard. Period-style details are quite fashionable these days. Maybe the answer to why wainscot persists is simple: When wood is used in the right measure as a wall covering, it makes a handsome addition to any room of the house.

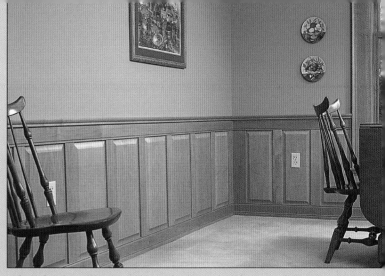

Prefabricated wainscot kits are one way to achieve the traditional look and feel of real wood wainscot, but without spending dozens and dozens of hours cutting and shaping in your shop. They are on the expensive side, however. Kits come in paint grade (left photo) and clear finish grade (right photo) in a variety of wood veneer types. Styles vary from traditional to contemporary. Pages 116 to 121.

Wainscot serves a couple of practical functions too. If you have damaged plaster or other kinds of wall blemishes to hide, wainscot is a perfect solution. Wainscot also serves as an attractive wall bumper against dents and dings caused by chairs, bed frames and other furniture.

If you'd like to recreate a period-style effect as well as add a distinctive wood feature to your home, add a wainscot project to your list of trim carpentry tasks. This chapter will teach you all the wainscot essentials you'll need to know. We'll outline the two principal styles of wainscot—tongue-and-groove and frame-and-panel—then walk you through the process of installing each type from start to finish. If you appreciate the look of frame-and-panel wainscot but aren't ready to commit the time and effort to building and installing it, consider a prefabricated system that even the occasional handyman can hang successfully.

Whichever wainscot style and finish you choose, keep in mind that solid-wood wainscot will be sensitive to high-moisture areas of your home. If you install wainscot in a bathroom, porch or basement, be sure to apply the finish to both the front and back sides before you install it. Wainscot finished only on the "show" side could absorb more moisture through the back than the front, causing it to buckle or warp. Do not install wainscot directly to block or poured concrete basement walls where moisture problems are common. Finish these walls with a plastic vapor barrier, insulation, framing or furring and wallboard first, then add the wainscot.

This chapter includes:
• Tongue-and-groove boards (pages 100 to 105)
• Prefabricated, solid panel kits (pages 116 to 121)
• Custom-built wainscot panels (pages 106 to 115)

Options for installing backer boards

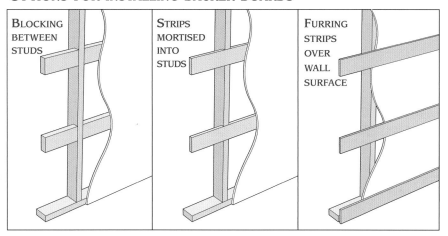

| BLOCKING BETWEEN STUDS | STRIPS MORTISED INTO STUDS | FURRING STRIPS OVER WALL SURFACE |

Backer boards provide added nailing surfaces for wainscot installation. When possible, install them prior to attaching the wallcovering, either by fastening 2 × 4 blocking between wall studs (left) or by cutting mortises for nailer strips into the wall studs (middle). Nailing strips can also be attached over wallcoverings (right), but it will cause the wainscot to project further into the room.

Cap and base options for wainscot

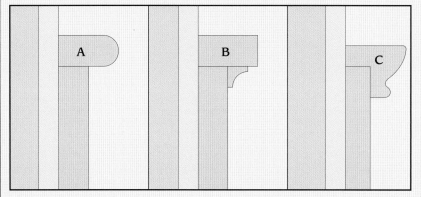

Cap rails are almost always installed on wainscot. More often than not, the caps are significantly wider than the wainscot, creating a small ledge. Option "A" in the illustration above can be milled easily in your shop, using a router. Option "B" is simply a strip of wood laid flat on the top of the wainscot, with cove molding attached in the seam. Option "C" is premilled wainscot cap molding, generally supplied with wainscot kits.

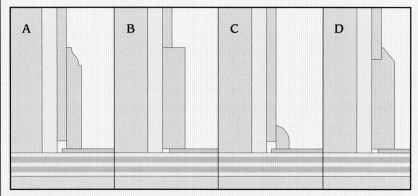

Basemolding of some type is almost always used with wainscot. Option A: Attach conventional basemolding over the wainscot. Option B: Attach basemolding to wall surface and butt bottoms of wainscot against basemolding. Option C: Cover gap at floor with base shoe only. Option D: Rabbeted base molding supplied with wainscot kit.

Preparing walls for wainscot

Wall studs are spaced too far apart to provide adequate nailing surfaces for some types of wainscot, particularly tongue-and-groove wood strips. Prior to installation of the wainscot, it's a good idea to install some form of solid nailing backer to the walls in the project area.

More than likely, your walls are covered with wallboard or plaster already. If they aren't and the wall framing is still accessible, the process for installing backer is relatively easy and quick. One option for backer is to nail lengths of 2 × 4 blocking between the wall studs to span the stud bays. You'll need one row of blocking positioned along the wall at the top of the wainscot and a second row located midway between the top row and the floor. Snap a level chalkline on the wall studs to mark each row of blocking. Fasten the blocking pieces by toenailing or screwing them at an angle into the studs. You can orient the blocking so either the narrow edge of the 2 × 4s or the faces are flush with the front edges of the studs. Either way will work, but the larger faces will provide more nailing surface.

If you are adding backer to an exterior wall with insulation between the studs, 2 × 4 blocking may take up too much space and compress the insulation. In this case, make the backer rows with

NOTICE: It is a code violation in most regions of the country to install wood wainscot directly to wall framing without a layer of wallboard or plaster in between. Wallboard and plaster serve as fire barriers, delaying the time it takes a fire to enter wall cavities and travel upward to other floors or the roof. Wood wainscot cannot be made into a suitable fire barrier. Check your local building codes before installing wainscot directly to wall framing.

long 1 × 4 nailing strips. You'll need to install the 1 × 4s flush with the edges of the studs so the wall-board will lay flat. To do this, hold the strips of 1 × 4 in place against the studs and mark the top and bottom edges onto the studs. Plan for two horizontal rows of backing just as you would with blocking. Cut across the studs at these reference marks with a circular saw set to a cutting depth of ¾ in. Remove the waste between the saw cuts on each stud with a chisel and hammer to form shallow mortises for the blocking. Then nail or screw strips of blocking in the mortises. Arrange the nailing strips so their ends are located in the mortises.

If wallcoverings are already in place, you can cut and remove strips of wall covering where the rows of blocking will go, then install the blocking and patch the openings with wallboard. An easier option is to install the backer boards directly over the wallcovering. Use ½-in. plywood or MDF cut into strips to make the blocking. Position strips at the top, center and bottom of the wainscot installation area, attaching them to the wall studs.

When wainscot meets casing...

Three methods for retaining your reveal when wainscot increases the thickness of your wall surface.

Wainscot should create a reveal where it meets window and door case moldings. Reveals help to hide the window/casing joints, while tying the wainscot and casings together visually. The setback from the face of the casings to the wainscot should be at least ⅛ in., but preferably a bit more.

If the wainscot you are installing (including any backer boards) is the same thickness or thicker than the room's window and door casings, you'll have to modify the casings in one of several ways to create a sufficient reveal. One option you might consider is to replace the case moldings with thicker case molding (See *Option No. 3,* lower right).

If you can't find suitable thicker casings, a second alternative is to install backband moldings around the outside edge of the casing to build up its thickness (See page 68). One-inch-square strips mitered at the corners will suffice for most picture-frame style mitered casings. (See *Option No. 2,* middle right).

Another solution is to fur out the case molding with spacer strips between the casing and the wall surface (See *Option No. 1,* upper right). Since they will be visible, the spacer strips should run continuously at the edge of the casing area, and preferably be made of the same wood type as the case molding. You'll also need to add jamb extensions at the inside edges of the casing (unless you make the spacer strips exactly the same width as the casing). For more on making jamb extensions see pages 48 to 49. You may need to replace the apron with one made from thinner stock so the stool can overhang the apron evenly.

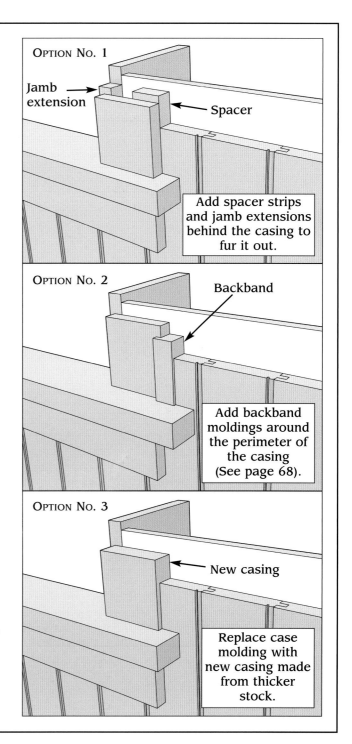

OPTION NO. 1

Jamb extension

Spacer

Add spacer strips and jamb extensions behind the casing to fur it out.

OPTION NO. 2

Backband

Add backband moldings around the perimeter of the casing (See page 68).

OPTION NO. 3

New casing

Replace case molding with new casing made from thicker stock.

Tongue-and-groove wood strips can be used to make inexpensive wainscot that's loaded with charm.

Tongue-and-groove wainscot

If you've ever installed a hardwood floor, think of tongue-and-groove wainscot as the wall counterpart to a wood floor. It consists of a series of narrow wood boards butted together vertically and detailed with a top cap to hide the end grain of the boards.

Each strip of wainscot is milled at the factory like flooring, with a tongue running along one edge and a matching groove along the other edge. As wainscot is assembled on a wall, the tongues and grooves interlock from board to board, which helps to align the wainscot as well as hold it flat. Nails are driven at an angle through each tongue, and the flange of the groove on the next board hides the nailheads. This nailing system, called *blind nailing,* creates a finished surface that is almost entirely free of fastener heads.

Since tongue-and-groove wainscot is solid wood, it continues to expand and contract seasonally as

humidity levels change. The interlocking tongues and grooves also allow the boards to shrink slightly in drier months without opening up into gaps.

Traditional tongue-and-groove wainscot is decorated along the face edges of each strip with bevel, bead or fillet profiles. Wider wainscot boards may also be milled with a bead down the center. Once it's installed, the overall effect of this profiling will vary, depending on the spacing of the profiles. Wainscot with closely spaced beads and bevels is most authentic, but it tends to look "busier" than wainscot made with wider boards and fewer profiles. When the boards are laid together edge to edge, the profiles create shadow lines along the board edges. This effect helps hide gaps between the boards. If the edges were left square rather

TIP: Apply finish to the wainscot strips while all the tongues and grooves are accessible. Whether your finish will be primer and paint or stain and varnish, finish the "show" sides of the strips as well as the backs. This way the wainscot will absorb and release moisture more evenly, which will help keep it from warping.

than profiled, gaps would be much more noticeable.

Material options. Most lumberyards and home centers stock tongue-and-groove wainscot boards, but the selection may be limited. Stock thickness will vary from about 5/16 in. up to 3/4 in. Wainscot may be sold in random lengths, especially at a lumberyard where you'll likely buy it by the board foot. Your home center may sell wainscot by the linear foot instead, in 8-, 10- or 12-ft. lengths. For the consumer market, 5/16-in.-thick wainscot is a common find at home centers, and it often is sold generically as solid-wood paneling in shrink-wrapped bundles of 8-ft. lengths. If you can't find wainscot in a dedicated area of the store, look on the wood flooring racks instead.

Traditional tongue-and-groove wainscot was made of pine, fir or other softwoods rather than hardwood. This holds true for wainscot manufactured today. Better lumberyards may carry more than one grade of wainscot, ranging from clear to knotty, but more than likely it all will be made of softwood. Lumberyards that do custom milling work can make up tongue-and-groove wainscot in any wood species you like.

If your lumber outlet doesn't sell wainscot, another substitute for softwood wainscot is tongue-and-groove wood flooring. Flooring won't have the characteristic bead profiles like wainscot, however. You'll have to mill the edge profiles yourself on the router table or it will look like flooring. Even though hardwood tongue-and-groove wainscot isn't really authentic, it may lend a contemporary and novel look to your project.

Another option to wood tongue-and-groove wainscot is sheet paneling embossed with a simulated beaded face to look like wainscot. Often called beadboard paneling, the core may be made of MDF, hardboard or lauan plywood. Paneling will be the least expensive route to installing wainscot. The downside to paneling is that it tends to look like paneling, not real wood. The embossed face layer will be a thin wood veneer, plastic laminate or white melamine, and the beaded pattern will be shallower and cruder than you'll find on real-wood wainscot. The upside to paneling is that it is easier to install than wood strips. It's often pre-cut to standard wainscot heights, and it goes up very quickly with paneling adhesive and short paneling nails.

BEADED WAINSCOT BOARDS & PANELS

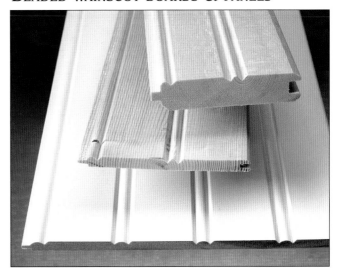

Tongue-and-groove boards suitable for wainscot range from 5/16 to 3/4 in. in thickness. In most cases, it's better to use thinner stock, which is cheaper and less likely to project out past your wall molding when it's installed. Some wider panels with intermediate beading also have tongue-and-groove edges.

Wainscot paneling is shaped with beaded profiles to look like tongue-and-groove boards. It is inexpensive, available in many styles and quality levels, and quick to install. Some is even pre-cut to length for use as wainscot. But it is still paneling, and even the best quality sheets don't quite manage to achieve the same look as solid boards.

Nailing tongue-and-groove boards

Tongue-and-groove boards (whether flooring or wainscot) are installed by "blind-nailing" through the tongues. Once the nailheads are recessed into the tongue with a nailset, the groove of the next board is slipped over the tongue, concealing the nail. Boards in illustration are viewed from above.

Nailing strips in stud cavity

1 Snap a level chalkline on the wall to mark the wainscot height (in this project, the top is 32½ in. above the floor). You'll use this line to align the top edges of the wainscot strips as you fasten them. NOTE: If you installed surface-mounted backer, you'll align the top ends of the boards with the top of the backer instead. In the project shown here, nailing strips have been installed in mortises in the wall studs, behind the wall surface. See pages 98 to 99.

2 Measure and cut the wainscot strips to length (¼ in. shorter than the chalkline height). Apply finish to all boards before installation—See page 100. Use a level to check the walls for plumb. If the wall is plumb and flat, you can go ahead and install the first strip. If the adjacent wall is out of plumb, you'll need to scribe the grooved edge of the strip to fit. Set the strip in place on the wainscot wall about ½ in. from the wall corner. Hold a level against the tongue edge and adjust the strip until it's plumb. Without moving the strip, set a compass to the widest gap between the wall corner and the grooved edge, then open it about ⅛ in. wider. Scribe the strip all along its length with the compass point following the wall corner. Trim off the scribe waste with a jig saw or block plane.

3 Nail the first strip (or outside corner piece) to the backer boards or nailing strips. Be sure the top end is aligned with your chalkline or with the top edge of the surface-mounted backer. Check with a level to make sure it's exactly vertical. Attach the strip at the top, center and bottom with finish nails driven through the tongue at about a 45° angle. Choose finish nails long enough to penetrate well into the backer. Drive the heads of the nails slightly below the surface of the tongue with a nailset. If you're using a pneumatic finish nailer, set the pressure regulator high enough to countersink the nailhead slightly—but not so high it shoots through the board.

Options for cornering with tongue-and-groove wainscot

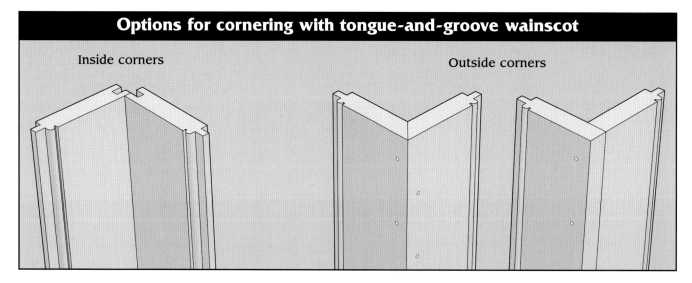

Inside corners

Outside corners

TIP: If you are installing the wainscot in fall or winter when the relative humidity is low, slip a couple of spacers about 1/16-in.-thick into the joints before nailing, then remove the spacers. These gaps will allow the wainscot to expand without buckling when humidity levels rise. Scraps of thin hardboard or two scraps of plastic laminate make good spacers.

4 Install successive strips, working your way along the wall. Slip the grooved edge of each strip over the tongue of the preceding strip and nail the tongues. Keep the boards plumb as you go, shifting the joints slightly before nailing to make adjustments as needed.

5 As you encounter obstructions, you'll need to cut the wainscot strips to work around them. The surest way to get your cutouts correct is to install strips as close as you can get to the obstruction (a receptacle box is shown here). Then, position the next strip on the opposite side of the obstruction to mark the top and bottom of whatever is in your way (Photo, above left). Position a short scrap piece of tongue-and-groove board above or below the obstruction, fitted over the tongue of the nearest attached strip. Mark the sides of the obstruction onto the scrap, then transfer the marks onto your workpiece. Make your cutout and attach the strip (Photo, above right).

NOTE ON RECEPTACLES. Building codes specify that the front edges of receptacle boxes are to be mounted flush with the finished wall surface. When you add wainscot to a finished wall, wainscot becomes the finished wall surface. To comply with code, you'll probably need to remove the existing receptacle boxes and install boxes that are flush with the wainscot surface. It's also possible to add plastic or metal box extensions to the existing boxes without removing them, but box extensions are not widely available. If you are not experienced with home wiring, hire a professional electrician for this part of the project.

(Continued next page)

6 When you reach door casings or window casings without stools and aprons, scribe and fit the wainscot strips around the casings instead of removing them. Be finicky about the fit of these casing joints; wainscot should fit against casings evenly and without creating gaps. See page 99 for more information on wainscot and window casings.

7 When you are within 8 to 10 boards of the other wall corner, measure the distance from the tongue edge of the wainscot to the wall corner. Fit as many boards together on the floor as will fill the remaining space. The goal is for the last board, called the "closing board," to be as close to full width as possible. If your layout suggests that the last board will only be a sliver of full width, fit the remaining board joints more loosely to take up the space of a narrow closing board. On the other hand, if the last board will be at least ⅔ its full width or wider, go ahead and install all the full width board up to the closing board. Then, scribe and fit the closing board. Measure from the wall corner to the closest wainscot strip at the top and bottom. Transfer these distances to the face of the closing board, measuring off the grooved edge (Inset photo). Then set the closing board in place with the tongue edge touching the wall corner.

8 Open a compass so the point touches the wall corner and the pencil intersects the top mark on the closing board. Without changing the compass setting, shift the bottom of the closing board forward or backward until the compass pencil intersects the bottom mark. Hold the closing board in this position, and scribe it from top to bottom. Trim along your scribe line with a jig saw set to a 2° or 3° back bevel. The back bevel will provide a bit of clearance so you can pivot the closing board into place in the corner. Plane off the beveled edge as needed for a better fit to the wall.

9 Nail the closing board to the backers or the corner wall studs. Since you've already removed the tongue, nail through the board face instead. If the wall adjacent to this corner will have wainscot also, drive nails close to the scribed edge so they'll be concealed by the first board of the adjacent wall. Drill pilot holes for the nails first to avoid splitting the board edge.

10 Begin installing strips on the adjacent wall, starting at the opposite end of the wall from the corner where the two walls meet. Repeat the process until all walls are covered.

11 Install a top cap to conceal the tops of the wainscot strips (See "Cap & base options," page 98). If the top cap is wider than the thickness of the door and window casings, notch the top cap so it fits around the casing by a distance equal to the amount it overhangs the wainscot. Execute your base treatment (See "Cap & base options," page 98).

The rectilinear shapes of frame-and-panel wainscot, especially when combined with a dark wood, give it a more sophisticated, formal appearance. Consider adding dark frame-and-panel wainscot to your dining room or formal living room. Flat insert panels are shown here.

Frame & panel wainscot

Instead of individual strips of wood nailed next to one another, frame-and-panel wainscot is built in wall-length components, usually off-site in the workshop. Each wall section consists of a long frame made up of horizontal rails and a series of vertical stiles. These rails and stiles wrap around wood panels, and the end result looks like a series of cabinet doors butted together. Once assembled, wall-length sections of wainscot are set into place and attached to the wall.

Design decisions. There are a number of possibilities for styling and configuring your frame-and-panel wainscot. The most common arrangement is to plan for a single row of panels on each wall with a top rail, bottom rail and stiles. If you decide to build wainscot taller than about 3 ft., you may want to incorporate more than one horizontal row of panels in your design, stacking the rows.

There are numerous ways to design the panels. *Raised panels* are the most common style for frame-and-panel systems. Each panel has wide, beveled edges all around the face with a large, flat field area in the middle. Raised panels will give your wainscot a traditional, Colonial effect. Usually, raised panels are made of solid wood. If the panels are narrow enough, you may be able to build them from single

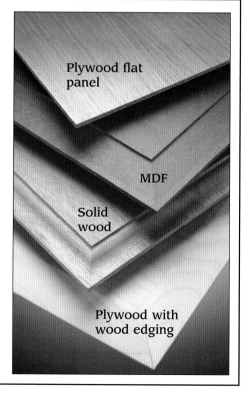

Materials

Frame-and-panel wainscot is generally made of hardwood and hardwood veneer plywood. The wood typically is finished with stain and a clear topcoat to enhance the wood grain. Darker woods like Honduras mahogany, walnut, cherry or teak are common choices for this wainscot style, as is wood with prominent figure, such as white oak. Painted frame-and-panel wainscot is also attractive, and it's typically built from paint-grade lumber like poplar, pine, birch or aspen. Painted panels are often made of medium-density fiberboard (MDF), a sheet-goods product made of finely ground wood pulp compressed under high pressure and heat. MDF is cheaper than paint-grade wood or cabinet-grade plywood, and it takes paint evenly because it has no noticeable pores or voids. MDF is also easy to cut and rout, and it produces crisp profiles and edges that need little sanding.

Plywood flat panel

MDF

Solid wood

Plywood with wood edging

boards. Otherwise you'll need to edge-glue several boards for each panel. Raised panels can be made out of veneer plywood too, but you can't bevel the edges without also exposing the inner plies. In this case, the beveled areas will need to be made of separate strips of solid wood and attached to the plywood "field" area with biscuits and glue.

Another option is to make your panels flat instead of raising the edges. Flat panels will project a more austere influence. Depending on the moldings you choose for the top cap and baseboard, flat-panel wainscot may be a better style choice if you want a more contemporary look. Flat panels can be built from solid wood, stain-grade plywood with an attractive face veneer or MDF covered with paint or wood veneer. To dress up a flat panel, you could cut a wide, shallow shoulder around the face frame to create a shadow line where the panel meets the framework.

For the framework, rails and stiles usually are made of solid wood, typically ¾ in. thick. Joints where the rails and stiles come together need to be strong, self-aligning and nearly invisible. To build the joinery, you'll need to employ one of several different woodworking joints suitable to the task. The most traditional joinery for rails and stiles is mortise-and-tenon, where the ends of the rails form long tenons that fit into mortises

ANATOMY OF FRAME-AND-PANEL WAINSCOT

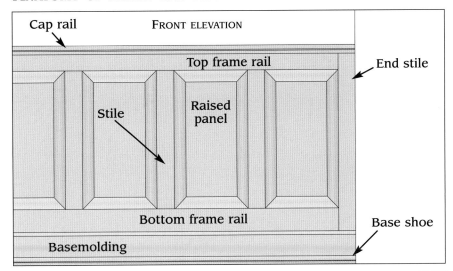

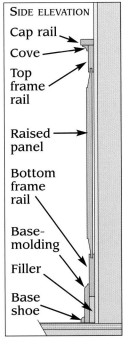

Frame-and-panel wainscot is composed of wood panels set into frames that are similar to cabinet face frames. The frames include horizontal rails and vertical stiles. The intermediate stiles fit between the rails, while the end stiles run from the top of the top rail to the bottom of the bottom rail. A cap rail and basemolding are also required.

in the stiles. Without a dedicated mortising machine, however, milling mortise-and-tenon joints for a room-full of wainscot is a tedious, time-consuming and exacting process. There are other sturdy (and easier) joinery options to choose from, including pairs of dowels or biscuits, tongues and grooves milled on the table saw or with a router, and the interlocking joint made by cope-and-stick router bits. One advantage to using cope-and-stick router bits for the rail and stile joints is that they also form an attractive profile around the inside frame edges next to the panels. This inner profile is a common detail in frame-and-panel wainscot. We'll use cope-and-stick router bits for the frame-and-panel wainscot built in this chapter (See page 112).

A few other areas available for detailing are the inside edges of the rails and stiles, where they fit around the panels. You can leave them square or dress them with routed profiles like coves, bevels, beads or ogees. A cap rail and basemolding round out the effect.

Building and installing wainscot yourself is a fairly major undertaking. Take plenty of time to do careful planning before you start, including creating a detailed and thorough plan drawing to eliminate most of the surprises that can happen.

OPTIONS FOR MAKING CORNERS

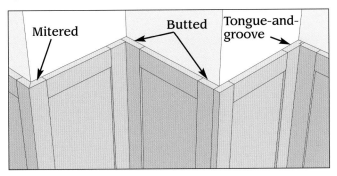

There are several ways to make inside and outside corner joints in frame-and-panel wainscot. The easiest is to simply butt the end stiles together. For these butt joints, make the stile that fits into the wall corner wider than the stile that butts against it. Make this extra width equal to the thickness of the stiles. Another approach for inside corner joints is to cut a tongue along the edge of one end stile and a groove into the face of the other end stile so the corner joint locks together. A tongue-and-groove joint will hide any gaps that form if the end stiles shrink, but the joint is trickier to build and fit. Use butt joints or miter joints where the end stiles of two wainscot sections meet at an outside wall corner.

Create a scaled elevation drawing for each project wall. Each drawing should include length and height dimensions for the wall, as well as the exact locations of its permanent features (receptacles, doors, windows, heat registers, cabinets), along with baseboard and cap designs. The completed drawing should also show you exactly how the wainscot section will look once it is installed so there are no surprises.

Making a layout plan & drawing

Drawing a detailed layout plan is the only way to develop a wainscot scheme for each wall that looks pleasing, is accurate enough to build from and harmonizes with the other walls in the room. The tough part of this layout work is that no two walls in a room will be the same. One wall may have an outside corner and a heat register, another wall will have a window and a door to contend with. A third wall might have a wall outlet that falls midway between a panel and a stile, which will need to be moved onto the panel or the stile alone.

Begin with the knowledge that you won't get the overall design right on the first try. Make your drawings on thin graph paper, and trace what you can from one version of a drawing to the next to save time. Sketch and re-sketch. Here are some pointers to help you with your layout:

• Generally, the top and bottom wainscot rails should appear to be about the same width. A 3- to 4-in. width for the rails is common. However, baseboard usually gets nailed to the bottom rail after the wainscot is installed, which covers up part of the bottom rail. This means one of two things: Either the bottom rail needs to be considerably wider than the top rail to keep its exposure above the baseboard equal to the top rail, or spacer blocking has to be added between the bottom rail and the floor.

• Stiles should be the same width on all walls, and they should be the same width or slightly narrower than the top and bottom rails.

• The panel widths may need to vary, even on a single wall, depending on how the panels fit around features like windows. Panels can be square or rectangular, and rectangular panels can be wider than they are tall or vice versa. In either case, if you're planning for the wood grain to

Create a second set of larger-scale drawings to verify other details once you've arrived at a wainscot design that works for all the walls. Among them, draw out your rail and stile joinery as well as the groove layout for the panels in the frames and any panel raising or other profiling you plan to do. Draw a detail of your end-stile corner joints as well, where two walls of wainscot meet.

show, orient the panels so the grain pattern runs vertically. This way the panel grain pattern will match the grain direction of other standing moldings in the room as well as the doors.

Start by drawing each wall accurately, including those features that will remain once the wainscot is added. Sketch your proposed baseboard and top cap next, then add the wainscot top and bottom rail as well as the outermost two stiles. These end stiles should extend all the way to the top cap, but the intermediate stiles should butt against the rails. With this done, you'll know the rough field area you have to work with for laying out the intermediate stiles and panels. If the wall has a window, plan for the area below the window to have one or two panels that completely fill this area. Align the ends of the panel (or panels) under the window with the outside edges of the window casing, then run the stiles up the sides of the window to the top rail, finishing this area. If the wall has a standing heat register, consider designing a baseboard that, when combined with the bottom wainscot rail, will be taller than the register. This way, the cutout for the register will be limited to the bottom rail and baseboard area rather than projecting up into a panel area, which would be more complicated to build.

For those blank areas that remain on the drawing, divide up the space with panels and stiles. Try to keep the stiles the same width, and shift the stiles around until the panel widths match. Take into account the location of electric outlets. If your drawing shows that an outlet will break both a panel and a stile, you should consider moving the outlet left or right during installation so it falls completely over a stile or a panel (See pages 122 to 123). Panels that must fill narrow spaces, such as those between a door and a close adjacent wall, will be narrower than those in the larger field area. This is unavoidable. If the space is too narrow for a panel here, fill the space with a wide stile and top cap instead.

As you are planning the proportions and number of panels per wall, keep in mind that the width of your panels will influence the materials and construction process you'll need to use to build them. Try to economize building materials where you can, and consider the physical limitations of the lumber available to you. If, for instance, the panel width exceeds 8 in. or so, and you plan to build the wainscot from hardwood in a clear finish, it will be difficult to find lumber wide enough to build the panels from a single piece of stock. You'll need to create blanks for the panels from more than one board, which will add time and effort to your building process. Panel width won't matter, of course, if the panels will be made of plywood or MDF, which can be any width up to 4 ft.

With these pointers in mind, take each wall drawing as far as you can to a final stage. Then compare the panel proportions you've determined for each wall. It's not necessary that the panel widths match around the room. This is very difficult to do. What's more important is that the proportions of the panels in the room are uniform overall. If the panel widths vary by even several inches from wall to wall, they'll still look like they are the same width to your mind's eye. One way to make this balancing process easier is to start with more stiles per wall and narrower panels. Just be sure that all the intermediate stiles around the room are the same width. The stiles on the ends of each wainscot section may need to be somewhat wider than the rest to allow for scribing. See the detail drawing, page 107, for an example of how stiles should intersect at inside wall corners.

Story poles

To help avoid mistakes, carpenters and cabinet builders often use simple tools called *story poles*. Story poles are straight lengths of scrapwood used for marking and labeling part dimensions and locations. You use them to transfer the important dimensions of your wall drawings as well as actual wall features into full-scale. The dimensions are represented on the poles by short reference marks and part names—no numerical measurements. For each wall of wainscot, you'll need a pair of story poles, one that charts the wainscot and wall features horizontally and another to mark important vertical dimensions. Make your story poles from any long, straight scrap. The horizontal story pole should be as long as the wall. Bevel both ends so the pole fits snugly into the wall corners.

There are two kinds of markings that belong on wainscot story poles. One set of marks are plotted onto the story poles using your scale drawings and a tape measure. These reference marks lay out the exact locations of rails and stiles on the wall. Other marks to add are locations of windows, doors, electrical outlets, heat registers and any other wall features that will impact the wainscot. Chart these wall features with the story poles held in place on the wall.

HOW TO MARK STORY POLES

Horizontal story poles (Above). For convenience sake on longer walls, make the horizontal story pole out of two shorter lengths of scrap that will overlap by 1 ft. or so when held together. Tradespeople often call these pinch sticks. Hold the two sticks where they overlap, and slide them apart until the opposite ends touch the wall corners. Then clamp or screw them together at the overlap to mark the full wall length. This way, you can take the strips apart for easier transport, then reassemble for use.

Vertical story poles (Right). Make the vertical story pole about 1 ft. longer than the wainscot height. To prepare the vertical poles for plotting reference marks, hold each one against the wall, so it is plumb and the bottom end is about ½ in. above the floor. Mark the poles where they cross a wainscot top reference line on the wall, and label this mark. Marking the vertical poles at the level line indexes them all from the same height. With the wainscot height established, proceed to plot marks for the top rail, bottom rail, any intermediate rails, the vertical locations of electrical outlets and the bottom edge of window sill casings.

Cutting profiles for raised panels

Making your own panels for frame-and-panel wainscot is mostly a router table task. There are several bits that can do the job. Here are a couple of the most useful.

Panel-raising bits (See photos, right). Many woodworkers will argue that the safest and cleanest way to raise a panel is to use a panel-raising router bit. There are two categories of panel-raising bits: horizontal and vertical. Horizontal panel-raising bits cut their profiles with the workpiece face-down on the router table. With vertical panel-raising bits, the workpiece is fed through the bit on-edge.

Cope-and-stick bits (See page 112) are commonly used in production cabinet-building for making door joints. The advantage to using these bits is primarily one of efficiency. In only two bit set-ups, the bits perform three functions: They cut the rail and stile joint, mill a decorative profile around the inside edges of the rails and stiles and cut a groove for housing a panel. The coping bit, which cuts the stub tenon for the joint, is commonly called a rail cutter. The sticking bit—or stile cutter—routs the groove and makes the decorative profile. Some manufacturers offer a single bit that accomplishes both cope and stick functions by rearranging the order of the cutters and bearings on the shank. Because of the cutting load demanded by these bits, they're better suited for variable-speed routers rated at 2 HP or more.

Horizontal panel-raising bit. Horizontal bits have two or three large carbide-tipped cutters oriented horizontally around a ½-in.-dia. shank. They're available in several sizes and bevel profiles, but 2½ in.-dia. bits are most common. Some have built-in anti-kickback features to make cutting safer. Because of their size and mass, horizontal bits should only be used at low speeds with a router rated at 2¼ HP or more. Raising a panel with a horizontal bit involves milling the bevel profile against a router fence with the panel oriented face-down on the router table. Make the bevel cut in several passes of increasing depth to avoid kickback. Never raise a panel freehand with a horizontal bit.

Vertical panel-raising bit. Vertical panel-raisers have two carbide cutters arranged vertically like a straight bit. Their geometry makes these bits smaller and lighter than horizontal bits, so they can be used safely in single-speed routers down to 1½ HP. Unlike horizontal bits, vertical bits have no pilot bearing, so they must be used on the router table in conjunction with a fence. Panels are fed on-edge or end past the bit, so the router fence needs to be tall enough to keep the panel from rocking as it's cut. Cutting the bevels with these bits should also be done in several passes, moving the fence further away from the bit with each pass.

Making raised panel inserts on a table saw

Raised panel inserts can only be made from solid wood—generally, ¾-in.-thick stock. (If you are painting the panels, you can make them MDF, however.) In almost all cases, that means you'll have to edge-glue boards together to get material that's wide enough to make the raised panels. Once you've glued-up the stock and cut it to size, you can cut the raised panel edge profiles with a router, but many woodworkers prefer to shape the edges on a table saw. This is a fairly simple approach.

HOW TO CUT EDGE PROFILES FOR RAISED PANELS USING A TABLE SAW

1 Edge-glue enough ¾-in.-thick boards to make workpieces for each panel. Arrange the glued-up boards so their wood grain will run vertically when the panels are installed. Be sure to joint the mating edges of the boards to get smooth seams. Structurally, it's not necessary to use biscuits, splines or dowels to reinforce the glue joints, but you may want to use them to help with alignment. Cut the glued-up panels to size—you'll likely need to use a circular saw and straightedge to make the cross-cuts, but they can be ripped to width on a table saw.

2 Bevel-cut the edges of the panel to create the raised panel effect. Ideally, the cuts will start ¼ in. in from the inside edges and exit the front face in mid-kerf, creating a slight reveal. Attach a tall, auxiliary wood fence to the table saw fence. Also clamp a fence guide to the panel to ride along the top of the auxiliary fence. Practice cutting with test pieces of ¾-in. stock until you've found the combination of blade height and bevel that makes the desired cut (a 3-in. cutting height with a 10° bevel is shown here).

Fence guide

3 Once you have established the best blade set-up position, rest each panel flat on the saw table, up against the auxiliary fence. Clamp the fence guide to the panel and feed the edge through the saw blade. The top of the blade should just break the outer face of the workpiece.

4 Cut all four edges of all panels the same way. It's important to keep the panels flat against the auxiliary fence at all times. Lightly sand the cuts smooth.

1 **Complete a detailed plan drawing (See pages 108 to 109).**
Rip and cross-cut the rails and stiles to size. Cut same-length parts, such as intermediate stiles, so their lengths match precisely (check them against a story pole—page 109). Remember to factor in the amount of extra length you'll need on the ends of the intermediate stiles to build the frame joints. This length will depend entirely on the joints you've chosen for your project. In the project shown here, we used cope-and-stick router bits to make the rail/stile joints, requiring an extra 3/16 in. of material on each end of the intermediate stiles for cutting tenons. Cut wider end stiles if your room corners are not square and you'll need to scribe the panel assemblies to fit. Label the rails and stiles clearly, according to your plans.

2 Build the frame joinery and cut grooves for the panels. Again, the tools, set-ups and sequence of steps required to make these joints and grooves will be determined by the choices you've made in your wainscot design. Whichever joints you build, a good depth for the panel grooves is ½-in. Since we used cope-and-stick router bits for the wainscot shown here, we started by cutting stub tenons on the ends of the rails and intermediate stiles using a piloted coping bit in the router table. Make a test cut on scrap of the same thickness before routing the rails and stiles. To make these cuts safer and minimize end-grain tearout, back up the cope cuts by guiding the rails and stiles with a miter gauge outfitted with a sacrificial fence. Or, use a piece of square scrap stock as a makeshift miter gauge instead.

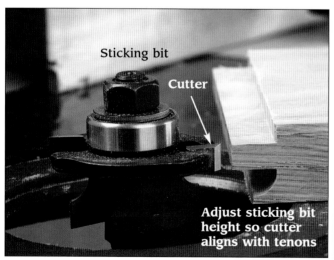

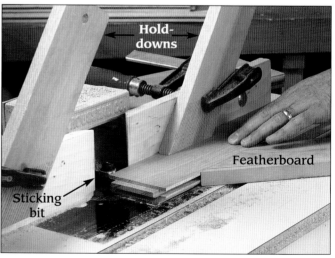

3 Once the coped tenons are cut, install the sticking bit in the router table to cut the mating pieces of the frame joints, as well as the grooves for the panel inserts. Adjust the bit height until the cutter that makes the groove lines up with the tenons on the parts you've already cut (Photo, left). Set the router fence so it lines up with the pilot bearing. Then make a test cut on scrap and check the fit of the rail and stile joint. Once you're satisfied with the set-up, mill this sticking profile along the full length of the following part edges: the inside edges of the top and bottom rails, both edges of any intermediate rails, both edges of the intermediate stiles and the inside edges of the end stiles. Make these cuts with the workpieces positioned face-down on the router table. Use featherboards and hold-downs to secure the workpieces.

5 Make the panel inserts. Our design called for flat, ¼-in. thick panels cut from oak plywood, so making them was simply a matter of cutting the panels to size on a table saw, based on the measurements we took in step 4. If you are using raised panels in your design, see pages 110 to 111.

4 Dry-fit the rails and stiles together to form the wainscot frames. First, clamp the horizontal story pole (See page 109) to each top and bottom rail and mark the locations of the stiles onto the rails. Then, assemble the rails and stiles on a large flat worksurface, aligning the stiles on your rail reference marks. Clamp the frame parts together. Verify that each panel opening is square. Measure the panel openings plus the depth of the grooves to determine the actual dimensions needed for the panels.

6 Sand the rails, stiles and panels smooth to prepare for finishing. Then dry-assemble the frames and panels to check the fit of the parts. Apply finish to the frame parts and panels prior to final assembly. Do not get finish materials on the mating ends of the rails and stiles—finish will prevent a good glue bond.

7 Assemble the wainscot sections with glue and clamps, gluing only the rail and stile joints. If the panels are solid wood, keep glue out of the panel grooves to allow for panel movement. Glue up the parts working from the center of the frame outward to the ends. Reserve one of the two end stiles in each frame if you intend to scribe it to fit.

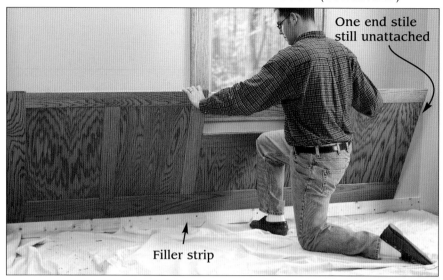

One end stile still unattached

Filler strip

8 To conserve oak, our plan called for the installation of 1 × 4 pine filler strips at the bottom of each panel location, where it will be concealed by basemolding anyway. We cut a filler strip to length and set it in place, measuring up to the reference line in several spots to make sure the line and the strip were parallel. Then, we nailed the filler strip to the sole plate in the wall framing. If you haven't allowed for the height of the filler strip in your plan, set the panel section in place and shim beneath it until it is level with the reference line. The wainscot section is set directly onto the filler strip. Shift the panel so the attached end stile is snug in the corner and press the section flat against the wall.

9 Scribe and trim the loose end stile so it will fit the opposite wall corner. First, measure the distance from the wall corner to the ends of the top and bottom rails. Transfer these two distances to the face of the end stile, measuring from the grooved edge.

10 Set the loose stile against the wainscot so the stile's flat edge touches the wall corner. Open a compass so the point touches the wall corner and the pencil intersects the top reference mark on the stile. Without changing the compass setting, shift the bottom of the stile forward or backward slightly until the compass pencil intersects the bottom mark. Hold the stile in this position, and scribe it from top to bottom. Trim along your scribe line with a jig saw set to a 2° or 3° back bevel. The back bevel will provide a bit of clearance so you can pivot the stile into place in the corner.

11 Before attaching the wainscot to the wall, mark and cut openings for wall outlets or any other wall features that need to pass through the wainscot. At this point, outlet boxes should be removed from the wall in preparation for retrofitting to the wainscot (See pages 122 to 123). Lay the wainscot face-down on the floor to mark it for outlets. Clamp the horizontal story pole to the top rail so the scribed edge of the fixed end stile and the end of the pole align. Transfer the outlet reference marks on the story pole to the wainscot, and draw perpendicular layout lines down the back of the wainscot with a framing square. Mark the outlet heights on the wainscot by aligning the vertical story pole with these layout lines. Transfer the story pole marks onto the wainscot. Draw the outlines and make the cutouts with a jig saw.

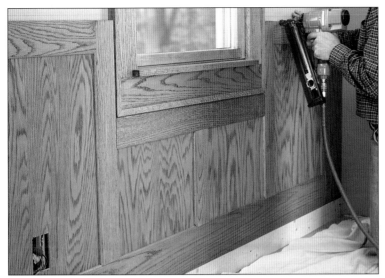

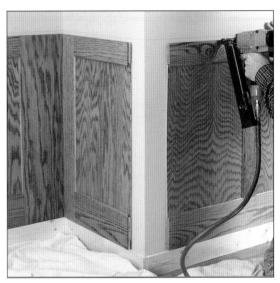

12 Reposition the wainscot on the wall and fasten it in place. First, apply glue to the ends of the rails that meet the loose end stile, and fit this stile to the wall. Install the wainscot with finish nails or wallboard screws driven into countersunk pilot holes. Choose fasteners long enough to penetrate at least 1 in. into the wall framing. It's really only necessary to attach the wainscot to the wall at the top and bottom rails. Locate the nails or screws high and low enough on the rails so they'll be hidden behind the top cap detail and the baseboard. Drive a fastener into each wall stud along the top rail and every 16 in. along the bottom rail, into the wall sole plate.

13 Install additional wall sections of wainscot using the same method, working outward from the first completed wall. For wainscot sections that meet at an outside wall corner, install the wainscot sections first, then trim and fit the loose end stiles to make the corner joint. The stiles could butt together here or be bevel-ripped to form a miter joint that hides the edge grain (See "Options for Making Corners," page 107).

14 Lock the corners together with glue and nails Once all the wainscot panels are in place, cut the cap rail to fit and install it with glue and nails, mitering inside and outside corners.

15 Cut and attach the basemolding according to your plan (See "Baseboard," pages 74 to 89). In the project shown here, we nailed the basemolding directly to the filler strip, then added base shoe molding. Install "cut-in" style receptacle boxes, make the wiring connections for the receptacles and install cover plates (See pages 122 to 123). Fill any nail holes with tinted wood putty, and make sure any glue squeeze-out is scraped (carefully) from corner joints.

Add frame-and-panel wainscot to any room in your home in a fraction of the time it takes to hand-build wainscot by installing a prefabricated kit. The kits are customized to include all the parts needed for your room.

Prefabricated Wainscot Kits

Until recently, the only way to add frame-and-panel wainscot to your home was to have it custom made or build it yourself from scratch. Not anymore. A number of companies now sell prefabricated wainscot kits that are easy for anyone with moderate skills to install.

The upside to installing a prefabricated kit is simplicity. All the decorative profiling on rails, stiles and panels is done for you at the factory, as well as the joinery required for assembling the parts. Prefab wainscot can be assembled on-site rather than in the shop,

with minimal cutting on your part. You can even buy your wainscot prefinished so it can be installed right out of the shipping cartons.

The downside to these conveniences is cost. Even the paint-grade product installed in the project shown here is on the spendy side.

Planning your prefab wainscot project

Wainscot kit manufacturers usually provide a planning guide that walks you through the process of laying out your project and estimating the materials you'll need. The process involves measuring your project walls and noting the locations of doors, windows and other permanent wall features. Log these measurements onto a simple wall sketch and on the wall and window layout worksheets supplied in the planning guide. The worksheets have scale drawings of each panel size assembled with stiles to help you determine which panel size will work best. You'll also find instructions for laying out panels and stiles below windows. Once you determine a suitable panel width and layout, draw your layout on the wall sketches to serve as an installation guide. Then, use the charts in the planning guide to create a materials list for the parts you'll need to buy. If you'd rather not do this layout and estimating yourself, most manufacturers offer design services to do the planning work for you.

Preliminary work. Walls are rarely flat in any
room. You'll have the best success installing this wainscot if, before installation, you flatten wall surfaces in
the project area. Check walls for flatness with a long
level or straight board held on-edge both horizontally
and vertically. Be most concerned with dips and bumps
that occur along the wall at the 32- or 36-in. top cap
height. The top cap that comes with the wainscot is
notched to fit over the top rail, but it provides no extra
material along the back edge for scribing to uneven
wall surfaces. If the top rail doesn't fit flat against the
wall beneath the top cap, gaps will form between the
cap and wall.

The best way to deal with dips and bows in the wall
is to apply a skim coat of joint compound to the walls
in the low areas. Feather out the compound above the
project area so it blends in with the rest of the wall.
Sand, prime and paint the walls before you install the
wainscot. If the wall in the top cap area is relatively
flat but the lower portions of the wall undulate, you
can build up the low spots with joint compound or glue
thin shims to the backside of the wainscot parts as you
install them. Whichever approach you take, the goal is
to install the wainscot so it creates a flat surface.

Remove window and door casings if your installation
kit includes casings and backband moldings. Replacing
your existing casing allows the backband to create an
attractive reveal next to the wainscot. The casings will
also match the wainscot. If you'd rather keep your
existing moldings and finish the wainscot to match, the
casings may still need to be removed temporarily, retro-
fitted and reinstalled after the wainscot is attached.

Finally, move any receptacle boxes on the wall that
will not fall completely within a panel or stile area.
Otherwise, the outlet cover plates will not fit flush
against the wainscot. See pages 122 to 123.

HOW TO INSTALL PREFAB WAINSCOT KITS

1 Locate the wall studs in the project area for nailing the bottom and
top rails in place. Use an electronic stud finder, or drill a series of
small holes in the project area to find the studs. Draw a plumb line
from the floor to just above the top cap and mark the stud centers.

2 Establish the height of the bottom rail and mark it on each project
wall. First, find the highest point of the floor along the project wall
or walls, using a long level or a straight board. Set a piece of bottom
rail against the wall at this high point and make a reference mark ¼ to
½ in. above the top of the rail. As long as the floor doesn't drop more
than ½ in. from the high point of the floor, you'll use this reference
mark as the height of the bottom rail. Draw or snap a level line along
each project wall to mark the top edge of the bottom rail. For floors
that drop more than ⅝ in., install the bottom rail against the floor at
the high point.

3 Apply finish to the "show" side of all the wainscot parts while their surfaces are still accessible. For paint-grade wainscot, prime the panels, then brush one coat of paint onto all the parts. Stain-grade wainscot can be finished completely at this stage with stain and clear finish. When sanding the parts, go lightly so you don't sand through the thin surface veneer.

4 Attach the bottom rail, starting from an inside corner. If the bottom rail will meet the bottom rails of adjacent walls, miter-cut the rail at 45°. For single walls, scribe and trim the end of the first rail. Cut scarf joints where one strip meets another strip along the wall. Align the top of each strip with the reference line. Attach with 8d finish nails or 2½-in. pneumatic nails. Nail and glue miter and scarf joints.

5 Fit and attach an end stile in a wall corner. The process for laying out the first end stile is somewhat round-about, but it will ensure that the end stiles on each wall are roughly the same width. First, find the center of the wall along it's length, and mark this point. The center of each project wall should split either a stile or a panel, depending on the wall length and panel width. Beginning at the center of the wall, dry-fit the panels and stiles out to the first end stile, taping the parts to the wall. Arrange the panels and stiles so they fit together as tightly as possible.

6 Locate and cut holes in the panels or stiles for receptacle boxes and phone jacks. Hold the panel or stile next to the outlet and mark the part from the bottom and side to locate where to lay out the cutout. Connect the reference marks on the back side of the panel or stile with a framing square to draw the shape of the receptacle box cutout. Cut the openings with a jig saw—jig saws cut on the upstroke, so cut the panels in a face-down position to prevent tear-out.

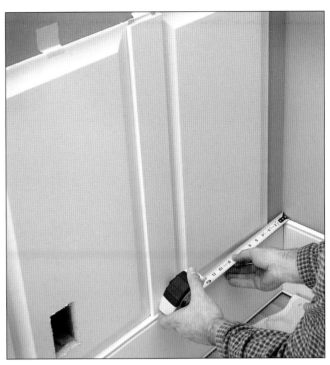

7 When you reach the end stile, measure the distance from the last panel to the wall corner and add ⁵⁄₁₆ in. to allow for the joint over-lap. If the adjacent wall is plumb and flat, rip one of the 10-in.-wide stiles to this width. If the wall corner is out of plumb, rip the stile about ½ in wider than necessary. Then, scribe the edge to fit (See Steps 9 to 11, page 114). You can also skip scribing if the edge of the end stile will be hidden behind the end stile of an adjoining wall.

8 To attach the end stile, apply a few dabs of construction adhesive along the back of the stile, set the stile in the bottom-rail rabbet and press the stile against the wall to seat it in the adhesive. Check the other edge of the stile for plumb before the adhesive sets.

9 Install panels and standard stiles, working toward the opposite cor-ner. Affix the parts to the wall with construction adhesive only. As you fit each part, tap the leading edge with a wood block and hammer so the parts fit snugly. Periodically check your work with a level. Install only enough panels and stiles to fit beneath one section of top rail.

10 Attach sections of top rail to the wall as you complete installation of panels and stiles up to the rail-length amount. Fit each length of top rail over the panel and stile tongues, and nail the top rail to the wall studs with 8d finish nails or 2½-in. pneumatic nails. Fit the ends of the top rail into the wall corners with either miter joints or end scribes, just as you did the bottom rail. Cut scarf joints and glue and nail one top rail strip to the next. To keep the top and bottom rail joints from becoming distracting, try not to have the joints line up with one another. This may mean cutting your first strip of top rail shorter to reposition the scarf joint.

11 For project walls with windows, begin the installation of panels and stiles under windows first, then work outward from the windows to the wall corners. Follow your window layout worksheets for arranging a horizontal panel (or panels) and stiles to fill the space between the window sill and the bottom rail. Trim 10-in.-wide stiles to fit around the window casing and cap the ends of the panel. Use either a 3- or 10-in. stile to fill the space above the panel and below the window casing. Install these parts with construction adhesive.

TIP: Use a section of the cap rail to make a window stool. You'll need to cut miters at the ends of the main section to create return corners (See "Mitered return horn," page 61). Notch the ends of the returns first to create "horns" on the stool. Then, cut the miters to fit.

12 Where two walls of wainscot form an outside wall corner, try to lay out and fit the end stiles so the rabbets on the edges of the parts form a butt joint. If one or both of the end stiles need to be narrower than full width, rip and fit the stiles together so you can use at least one of the rabbeted edges for the corner butt joint. If the stile needs to be wider, join two stiles with a scarf joint. Refer to your installation guide for other corner options.

13 Install top cap over the top rail. Miter-cut the cap molding for making inside and outside corner joints. Where one strip of cap molding meets another, fit the ends together with glued scarf joints. Lay out the scarf joints so they're staggered with any top rail scarf joints. Attach the cap molding with a bead of construction adhesive and 4d finish nails or 2-in. pneumatic nails. Drive the nails into wall studs, and locate the nails so they're hidden in the cap profile grooves.

14 Nail shoe molding to the bottom rail with 4d finish nails or 1½-in. pneumatic nails to hide the gap at the floor. Miter the inside and outside corner joints, and use glued scarf joints where the ends of the shoe moldings meet. Back-bevel the shoe molding where it meets heat registers. Since back bevels will expose the MDF inside the molding, cover the ends with adhesive-backed veneer tape supplied with the wainscot. Apply the veneer tape before you install the molding. Fill the nail holes with color-matched wood putty or spackle. Apply a second coat of paint to paint-grade wainscot. Install outlet boxes or box extensions, wire the receptacles and attach cover plates (See pages 122 to 123).

Moving electrical boxes

When installing wainscot, you'll often encounter situations where you must move electrical receptacles. Most building codes specify that the front edges of receptacle boxes are to be mounted flush with the finished wall surface. When you add wainscot to a finished wall, wainscot becomes the finished wall surface. To comply with code, you'll probably need to remove the existing receptacle boxes and install boxes that are flush with the wainscot surface. It's also possible to add plastic or metal box extensions to the existing boxes without removing them, but box extensions can be hard to find.

When planning a wainscot installation, you may also find that it makes more sense to relocate a box than to work around it.

HOW TO RELOCATE A RECEPTACLE BOX

1 First, shut off power to the circuit that feeds the wires in the box then remove the receptacle. Trim away enough wallboard around the box to determine how it is held in place. More than likely, the box is attached to a stud, either with a pair of framing nails on the top and bottom or by means of a metal plate that wraps around the front of the stud and nails in place. To remove the box, you'll need to cut through the nails or the supporting plate. Use a reciprocating saw with a metal-cutting blade or make the cuts by hand with a hack-saw blade. Be careful not to nick or cut through the wires.

2 If cutting the box loose is impractical, remove the wallboard around the box and pull out the nails that hold it in place. Once the box is free, loosen the cable connector screws (if any) that hold the wires tightly in the box. Pull the box out of the wall. Extend the cut-out in the wall covering to or make a new cutout to correspond to the new box location. Patch the wallboard.

3 After the wainscot is up, install a "cut-in" style receptacle box (See top photo, next page) and mount it so the front edges of the box are flush with the face of the wainscot. Reinstall the receptacle, making the necessary wire connections, and attach a cover plate.

Cut-in box types

Most boxes designed for retro-fit, called cut-in boxes, employ a system of toggles or wings that are drawn in tightly against the interior of the wall to hold the box in place. They are designed to be "free-floating" in that they

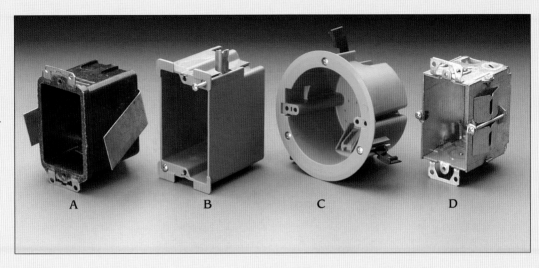

A   B   C   D

mount anywhere on the wall surface; many will not work properly if installed next to a wall framing member where the operation of the wings will be impeded. The types shown above include: (A) Thermoset box with metal tension straps; (B) PVC box with

metal flip-out wings; (C) PVC fixture box with plastic flip-out wings (used mostly for ceiling-mounted lights, but can be used for wall-mounted lights on high wainscot); and (D) metal box with screw-tightened compression tabs.

HOW TO INSTALL A BOX EXTENDER

1 Electrical box extenders can be installed after the wainscot is in place to "fur-out" the box so it is flush with the new wall surface—a requirement of most building electrical codes. With the power off, remove the old receptacle and insert the extender into the cutout in the wainscot panel.

2 Box extenders are slightly smaller than standard box sizes, so they fit into the box openings. This allows you to adjust the position of the extender simply by tightening screws threaded through the extender and into the matching screw holes in the box. Tighten until the front edges of the extender are flush with the wainscot surface, then connect the receptacle and install the coverplate.

PROJECT VARIATION:
Easy Fireplace Mantel

If you're attracted to the idea of building your own fireplace mantel structure but don't have the time or experience to undertake something as complex as the beautiful surround featured in this chapter, here's a nice compromise. This easier-to-build fireplace mantel is well-stocked with charm, and the process for making it is quite similar to the step-by-step project outlined on the following pages.

The surround pictured was built from solid red oak boards and moldings. If you're lucky, you'll find a board wide enough to make the broad top rail from a single piece of lumber. If you can only find narrow stock, it's a simple matter to glue up two or more boards to make up the required width. You also could substitute a piece of ¾-in. plywood.

~ Project designed by
Neal Barrett
~ Illustration created by
Gabriel Graphics
~ Photograph by *Carl Weese*

This lovely fireplace surround can be built using the same basic procedures and techniques as the more complex project featured on pages 125 to 133.

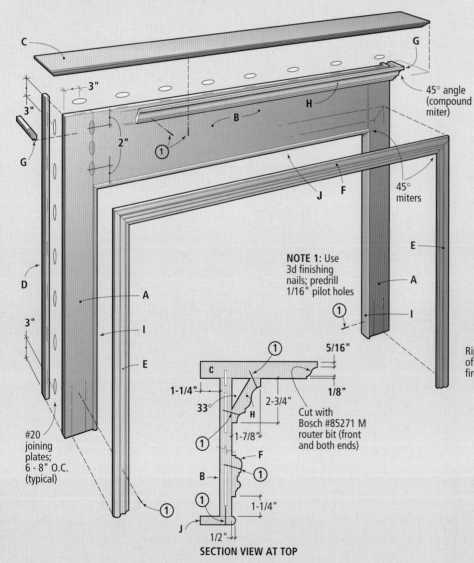

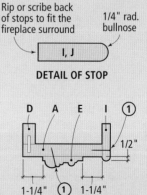

SECTION VIEW AT TOP

SECTION VIEW AT SIDE

DETAIL OF STOP

Whether called a "mantel" or a "fireplace surround," the trim pieces and shelf that are arranged around a fireplace can make a bold design statement that turns a purely functional part of your home into a showpiece.

Fireplace surround

Nothing sparks conversation like a crackling fire. For those times when there's no fire in the hearth, your fireplace can still be the focal point of the room if it's outfitted with an attractive fireplace surround. Aside from adding visual appeal, you might also want to replace your existing fireplace surround if you've just installed new casings or wainscot and the fireplace surround no longer matches the wood type or style of the rest of the trimwork. The fireplace surround we'll build on the next few pages is a project you can tackle with basic trim carpentry skills. You'll also need a table saw, power miter saw, router table and a jig for drilling dowel joints.

A couple of quick definitions: All of the woodwork that surrounds the opening of a fireplace is considered the *mantel*—not just the ledge that runs along the top.

The vertical, column-like trim pieces on each side of the firebox are called *pilasters,* and the horizontal surface immediately above the firebox is the *frieze.* Notice in the surround featured here that the frieze consists of three rails. The reason for the gaps between rails is to provide room for the rails to expand and contract across the grain—especially the wide center rail.

If you build this surround according to the dimensions given in the cutting list, the opening will measure 42 in. tall and 50 in. wide. Adjust the part lengths as needed to suit your fireplace size. Be sure to check the building codes in your area to see that these dimensions conform to setback regulations for attaching combustible material around a fireplace. Usually, there needs to be 6 to 12 in. between the firebox opening and the surrounding woodwork. Codes may also specify how far the mantel shelf must be kept away from the firebox opening. This distance may vary, depending on the amount the mantel shelf overhangs the firebox.

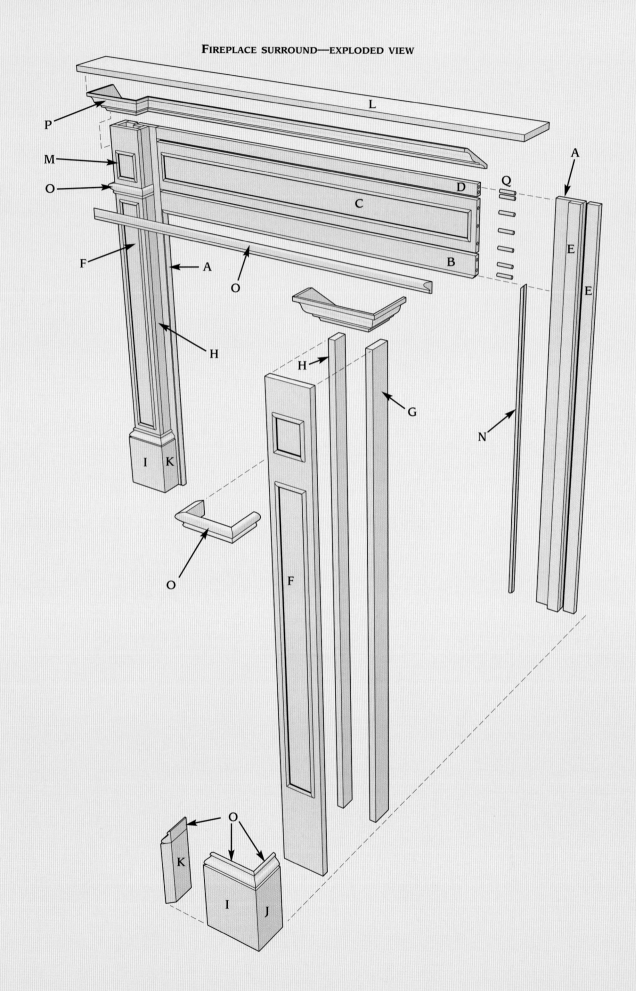

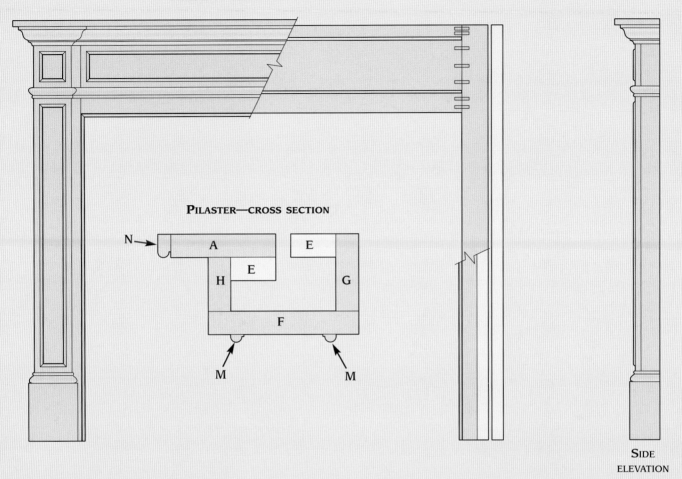

PILASTER—CROSS SECTION

SIDE
ELEVATION

CUTTING LIST-Fireplace Surround

KEY	No.*	Description	Size*	Material
A	2	Pilaster backers	$3/4 \times 3\,1/2 \times 53\,3/4"$	Oak
B	1	Frieze rail (bottom)	$3/4 \times 2\,1/2 \times 50\,7/8"$	Oak
C	1	Frieze rail (middle)	$3/4 \times 6\,1/2 \times 50\,7/8"$	Oak
D	1	Frieze rail (top)	$3/4 \times 1\,1/2 \times 50\,7/8"$	Oak
E	4	Pilaster cleats	$3/4 \times 1\,1/2 \times 53\,3/4"$	Pine
F	2	Pilaster faces	$3/4 \times 5 \times 53\,3/4"$	Oak
G	2	Pilaster outsides	$3/4 \times 2\,1/2 \times 53\,3/4"$	Oak
H	2	Pilaster insides	$3/4 \times 1\,3/4 \times 53\,3/4"$	Oak
I	2	Plinth faces	$3/4 \times 6\,1/2 \times 7\,1/2"$	Oak
J	2	Plinth outsides	$3/4 \times 4 \times 7\,1/2"$	Oak
K	2	Plinth insides	$3/4 \times 3\,1/4 \times 7\,1/2"$	Oak
L	1	Mantel shelf	$3/4 \times 6 \times 68\,3/4"$	Oak
M	30 ft.	Face Bead Molding	$7/16 \times 1/4" \times$ various	Oak
N	12 ft.	Edge Bead Molding	$7/16 \times 3/4" \times$ various	Oak
O	12 ft.	Panel Molding	$1\,1/16 \times 1\,3/8" \times$ various	Oak
P	8 ft.	Crown Molding	$9/16 \times 3\,1/4" \times$ various	Oak
Q	14	Dowel Pins	$3/8$ dia. $\times 2"$	Hardwood

* Length and quantity of parts depends on individual project dimensions.

1 Rip and cross-cut the pilaster backers and three frieze rails to size. Attach the frieze rails to the inside edges of the two backers with dowels and glue. Lay out the parts so the top frieze rail aligns with the tops of the backers and there are ⅜-in. gaps between the rails. Make the dowel joints by drilling ⅜-in.-dia. × 1-in.-deep holes in the ends of the rails and the edges of the backers, using a doweling jig. The narrow rails should have two dowels per end and the wide rail should have three. Then, spread glue on the dowels and the mating surfaces of the rails and backer, and clamp the parts together on a large, flat worksurface. NOTE: When gluing up the wide frieze rail, spread glue only to the outermost dowels. Leave the outer edges dry to allow for wood movement.

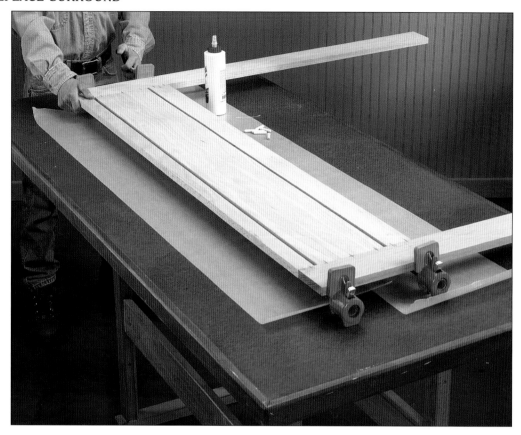

2 Install the frieze assembly on the fireplace wall. If your fireplace is surrounded by a wall with wood framing, locate and mark the wall studs first. Set the assembly in place so it's centered on the fireplace opening, and shim beneath the backers, if necessary, to level the top of the frieze. You may want to tape your level to the frieze for leveling to keep it from falling off as you work. Notice that the inside bottom corners of the backers will show once the pilasters are installed. If you've shimmed the assembly, use a compass to scribe the bottoms of the backers, then trim them so the frieze assembly stands level and tight to the floor without shims. Attach the assembly to the wall framing with 3-in. wallboard screws. Locate the screws along the pilaster backers and the top frieze rail so they'll be hidden once the pilasters are installed. If there are no studs located in the backer attachment areas, secure them to the wall with construction adhesive and molly bolts or screws driven into suitable wallboard anchors. To install the fireplace surround on masonry walls, use lead or plastic expanding anchors and screws instead of wallboard screws.

3 Cut the four pilaster cleats to size, and attach one cleat to each of the pilaster backers so the outer edges of the parts align. Fasten the cleats to the backers with glue and 1¼-in. wallboard screws.

4 Rip and cross-cut the pilaster faces, insides and outsides to size. Assemble both pilasters with glue and 6d finish nails or 2-in. pneumatic nails. Sand or lightly plane the joint smooth, if necessary, after the glue dries.

5 Attach the remaining two pilaster cleats on the wall. To determine the location of these cleats, set the pilasters in place on the backers so the inside piece of each pilaster rests against the cleat already attached to the backer. Draw a reference line on the wall down the outside of each pilaster, then remove the pilasters.

6 On the wall, draw a second set of lines ¾ in. in from the first reference lines to mark the cleat locations. Attach the cleats to the wall along these lines, driving the attachment screws into wall framing. If there are no studs located in the cleat areas, use construction adhesive and molly bolts or screws driven into suitable wallboard anchors.

7 Slip the pilasters over the cleats, and attach them by nailing through the sides of the pilasters and into the cleats. Use 6d finish nails or 2-in. pneumatic nails to fasten the pilasters.

8 Cut the plinth outsides, insides and faces to size. The grain pattern should run vertically when the plinths are installed. Bevel-rip one edge of the side plinth parts and both edges of the plinth faces at 45° so the plinths will form miter joints where they wrap around the pilasters.

10 Cut and nail strips of panel molding to fit around the pilasters (hiding the gap formed between the middle and bottom frieze rails) and around the top ends of the plinths. Use miter joints to join the moldings around the pilasters and either miter or cope joints to make the inside corner joints where the pilasters meet the frieze. Glue and nail the molding in place.

9 Install the plinths. First, dry-fit the plinth parts around the pilasters to be sure the miter joints will close tightly. Spread glue over the back faces of the plinth parts and along the mitered edges. Tack the plinth pieces to the pilasters with finish nails. To help hide some of the nails, nail at an angle down through the top edges of the plinths. Locate the other nails as close to the floor as possible.

11 Attach the mantel shelf: Rip and cross-cut the shelf board to size, and set it in place on top of the frieze and pilasters to check its fit to the wall. If the wall surface isn't flat and creates gaps along the back edge of the shelf, scribe and trim the back shelf edge to improve the fit. Be sure the mantel shelf over-hangs the pilasters evenly all around. Secure the shelf by nailing down through the shelf and into the pilasters and top frieze rail.

12 Cut and nail crown molding beneath the mantel shelf to form a decorative cornice. The crown molding also will help support the shelf. Follow the same technique for cutting the molding on a power miter saw as you would for installing crown molding at a ceiling (See pages 136 to 149). Cut and install the molding, starting at the frieze and working outward. Use cope joints for making the inside corner joints where the frieze and pilasters meet. Build the cope joints so the long center piece of crown molding butts against the pilasters, then cope the short inside pieces of crown that fit against the pilasters. Switch to compound miter joints for wrapping the crown molding around the pilasters. Spread glue along the miter joints, and attach all the molding pieces to the pilasters, shelf and frieze with 3d finish nails driven into pilot holes.

13 We detailed the pilaster faces and the inside edges of the surround opening with bead molding made to spec on a router table and table saw. If you aren't interested in milling your own moldings, you can bring the sizes and profiles shown here to a millwork/cabinetmaking shop and have them make it for you. Or, substitute a stock molding you like from your local lumber center. The face and edge bead molding called for in the cutting list have the same profile, but the thickness of moldings varies. Make the molding stock by routing both edges of a wide oak board on the router table with a piloted beading bit.

14 Rip the routed edges of the molding stock off on the table saw to cut the molding to size. Repeat this process to make more strips of molding. Change the saw fence setting to make the two thicknesses of molding required. Also cut strips of edge bead molding to fit around the inside edges of the fireplace surround.

15 Lay out the square and rectangular patterns on the pilaster faces for applying the face bead molding. Lay out and install face bead molding on the center frieze rail to form that decorative detail.

16 Miter-cut, glue and tack the face bead molding in place with 3d finish nails or brads. Cover all exposed nailheads with tinted wood putty or a putty stick, and ease sharp corners and edges of the fireplace surround with 180-grit sandpaper. Apply your choice of stain and varnish to complete the project.

Ceiling Trim

Unlike baseboard or window and door trim, ceiling trim doesn't serve the primary purpose of hiding gaps. The purpose of ceiling trim is almost entirely decorative, with the exception of those instances where the molding can conceal mechanicals like ductwork, plumbing or exposed wiring. From the standpoint of appearance, ceiling trim can dress up any room in the home, and it makes a graceful transition from walls to ceiling.

Ceiling trim looks particularly fitting in rooms that are trimmed with other traditional elements, like window stools and aprons or corner and plinth blocking. It can be painted to match the walls or ceiling, or painted

another color for contrast. Ceiling trim also can be stained to match the rest of the natural woodwork.

"Ceiling trim" is a broad category that breaks into two groups: those moldings that lay flat against walls and those "sprung" moldings that form an angle between the walls and ceiling, such as crown and cove molding. Flat ceiling moldings are usually nothing more than base molding installed against the walls with the profile facing downward. Usually, the edge that butts against the ceiling is hidden behind cove or quarter-round molding to conceal any gaps formed between the molding and the ceiling. Flat ceiling moldings are less common as a trim detail than sprung varieties, but they are much easier to install. For best appearance, choose flat moldings that are narrower than the base-board in the room and mimic or match the baseboard

Cornice options

Instead of installing plain molding, you can combine flat and sprung moldings in different configurations to form built-up ceiling moldings, commonly called "cornices." The illustrations shown here indicate a number of different cornice types you can build, along with the moldings that make them up. The benefit to a cornice is that it adds more sophisticated appeal than simpler ceiling molding schemes and creates a formal atmosphere in a room. If you have mechanicals to hide or wish to add recessed lights at the ceiling, a cornice also provides more hollow space than sprung moldings for hiding these items. Depending on the cornice scheme, you may be able to build some of it off the wall at a comfortable working height, then fasten the assembly in place in sections and hide the joints with other moldings.

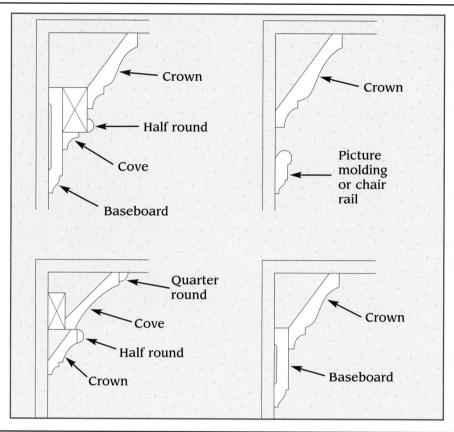

profile. Fit, cut and install them exactly as you would baseboard, with cope joints on the inside corners and miter joints at the outside corners.

Originally, sprung ceiling moldings were triangular in cross section, so the molding fit all the way into the ceiling corner, and the front face formed an angle to the ceiling and walls. But modern sprung moldings are milled from thinner boards, and the top and bottom edges are each cut at angles that lay flat against walls and ceilings. Once the molding is installed, it creates a hollow area behind it, which actually helps the molding conform to minor irregularities in the wall or ceiling.

Getting started

Installing ceiling trim will go much more smoothly if you take care of a number of preliminary tasks first. Running ceiling moldings around a room is similar in many ways to installing baseboard, but the joinery is more complex. Read the "Tips for installing baseboard" section, page 77, for a few pointers that also apply to ceiling moldings. Following are a few additional tips specific to ceiling moldings that will help you prepare for a ceiling molding project:

Buy extra molding. Ceiling moldings are sold as *running molding* in random lengths. Estimate the amount of molding you'll need for the job by measuring the perimeter of the room, then adding 20% more material to this total. NOTE: Cutting compound angle joints for sprung ceiling moldings creates more waste than other types of joinery. Depending on the orienta-

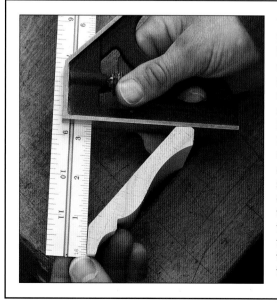

TIP: Determining sprung molding height. Measuring the actual height of a piece of crown molding will not yield the height measurements you need to find the amount of space it will occupy when installed. The best way to determine the installed height is to use a combination square. Place a piece of the molding into the square so the edges that will contact the wall and ceiling rest flush on the blade and head of the square. The distance from the bottom of the molding to the head is the installed height for the molding.

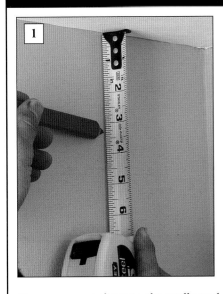

Even on newer homes, the walls and ceiling are seldom exactly level and square to one another. The best way to ensure that ceiling moldings are level all around is to create a level reference line to align the bottoms of the moldings, keeping them parallel to window and door trim.

1 Find the lowest point on the ceiling and measure down from that point to establish a layout line for the crown molding. The distance you measure should equal the height of the crown molding when installed (See TIP, previous page).

2 Use a water level or a laser level to transfer the line all around the room. Or, use a framing level to transfer the point to spots all around the room, then connect the points with a chalkline.

3 Measure the installed height of the crown molding upwards from the layout line in several spots. Look for any gaps greater than ¼ in. or so. Adjust the line upwards slightly if necessary (you may need to scribe the molding to fit against the ceiling if you adjust the line, however).

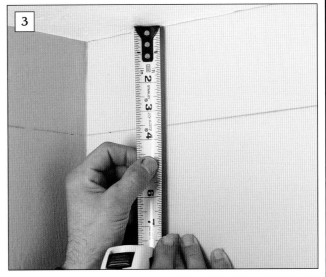

tion of the joint you are making, you'll routinely need to swing the saw in the opposite direction to create a mitered end that faces the correct way, which wastes material. Some of the compound joinery you'll make, especially miter joints for outside wall corners, will require more molding because the molding extends beyond the wall corners a distance equal to its width. It's also a good idea to have extra molding on hand for making preliminary mock-ups of each joint on scrap pieces. This way you can fine-tune your saw settings before committing to the final cuts. The mock joint pieces also will help you keep the orientation of the

moldings clear; keep these pieces handy for setting up your final cuts.

Apply the finish first. Stain and varnish or prime and paint all the strips of molding you plan to use before you begin the project. Don't forget to topcoat the backside of the molding as well as the face, which will help the molding absorb and release moisture evenly to keep it from warping.

Cut the moldings to rough length first. Get efficient use out of random molding lengths by cutting each strip you'll need to rough length first. Outside corners, made with compound miter joints, will require the most material. Allow 6 in. of extra molding for each end

Shim to fill gaps

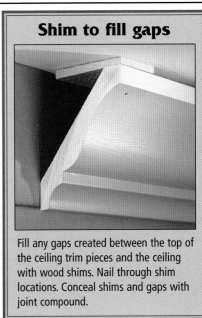

Fill any gaps created between the top of the ceiling trim pieces and the ceiling with wood shims. Nail through shim locations. Conceal shims and gaps with joint compound.

that will receive an outside miter. In general, cut strips at least 1 ft. longer than necessary to allow for test-cutting the end joints.

Mark stud and joist locations. Ceiling trim is nailed to wall studs, top plates and, in the case of sprung moldings, ceiling joists. Before installing trim, mark these framing members just outside the installation area. Use an electronic stud finder, or make a series of exploratory holes with a finish nail or small bit

chucked in a drill to pinpoint the location of the framing members. Drill exploratory holes where they'll be concealed by the trim. Mark the framing locations with light pencil marks or strips of tape.

Establish a general installation plan. Draw a bird's-eye view of the ceiling, identifying the type and orientation of each joint you'll need to make. Establish the installation sequence you'll follow. Even though you'll build sprung molding joints differently than flat base-

Sprung molding backing

OPTION: Install 2 × 6 nailers

OPTION: Install beveled nailing strips

Photos shown in cutaway for clarity

In order to install sprung ceiling moldings successfully, there must be solid nailing surfaces behind the walls and ceiling. Walls pose no problem because you'll nail the moldings to the wall studs and/or to the top plates next to the ceiling. Narrow sprung moldings can be nailed entirely to the wall framing, if necessary. Locating solid nailing surfaces can be more of a problem with ceilings. Where the wall is perpendicular to the ceiling joists, the joists serve as adequate nailing surfaces. When walls are parallel to the joists, however, you'll need to create nailing surfaces in these areas. One option is to fasten 2 × 6 nailers to span from cap plate to cap plate on opposing stud walls, cantilevering over the ceiling (See photo, above left). This option is only realistic in situations where you can access the joists from above, such as in an attic, or in new construction before the ceiling wallboard goes up.

Another alternative is to attach a pair of beveled nailing strips to the wall's top plate where the wall and ceiling meet (See photos, above right). First, mark the position of the molding on the ceiling and wall. Then, on a table saw, bevel-rip pairs of ¾-in.-thick plywood strips that will butt up to the backside of the sprung molding in the hollow area. The strip against the ceiling should butt against the wall and will be installed first. Size the strip that fits against the wall so it will butt against the bottom of the ceiling strip. Find the bevel angles for cutting the backer strips by holding a straightedge across the flat top and bottom edges of the sprung molding, then reading the angle formed by the straightedge and the flat back of the molding with a protractor. NOTE: When you cut the backer strips to length, be sure

those supporting moldings at inside corners won't interfere with the butted piece of the cope joint— the butted piece of molding needs to extend all the way into the wall corner.

To mount the strips, hold the ceiling strip in place against the ceiling with the aid of a helper, then position the wall strip tightly against the ceiling strip. Attach the wall strip to the wall studs with wallboard screws long enough to penetrate the wall studs by about 1½ in. Then drive wallboard screws into the corner between the two strips to secure the ceiling strip.

A third option for creating a continuous nailing surface along the ceiling is to incorporate a flat piece of basemolding or even a flat board into your ceiling molding scheme as the topmost element in the design. Mount the flat board or basemolding to the ceiling with molly anchors and long machine screws. Position the fasteners far enough in from the outside, exposed edge so the screwheads won't interfere with the placement of the sprung molding. Butt and nail the top of the sprung molding against this top flat element.

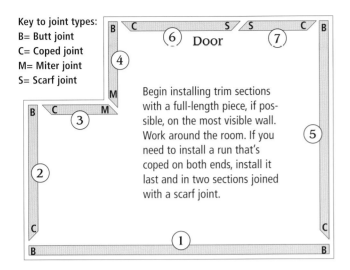

Key to joint types:
B= Butt joint
C= Coped joint
M= Miter joint
S= Scarf joint

Begin installing trim sections with a full-length piece, if possible, on the most visible wall. Work around the room. If you need to install a run that's coped on both ends, install it last and in two sections joined with a scarf joint.

board joints, the kind of joinery involved is the same—inside corner joints are made with cope joints, not miters. Outside wall corners will receive compound miter joints. Arrange the order of installation starting on the wall opposite the entry door (generally the most visible wall) and work your way around the room. Set up cope joints so the butted pieces of these joints are those you'll see most prominently, in case the joints open up over time. The gaps will be more noticeable when viewed from the side of the joint with the coped edge. Try to avoid ending the installation with a workpiece requiring cope joints on both ends, although this might be difficult to do. If this scenario is the case in your floorplan, make the last run of molding with two strips connected with a scarf joint.

Draw or snap reference lines. Crown and other sprung moldings don't provide much material along the top edge for scribing against ceilings that aren't flat. Consequently, you have two options for aligning the moldings with the ceiling. If the ceiling is flat and level, butt the moldings against the ceiling all around the room. For ceilings that sag, you'll need to locate the lowest point of the ceiling where it intersects the walls, then level all of the moldings to this point. Otherwise the moldings will follow the drift angle of the ceiling and meet out of alignment in the corners. This will make the joints tougher to cut and fit. In either case, the goal is to install the moldings level so they'll appear parallel to the head casings of doors and windows. The best way to accomplish the task is to establish a level reference line on the walls all around the room to align the bottom edge of the molding.

To create the level reference lines, first check the ceiling for level using a carpenter's level held against a long straightedge, such as a 2 × 4 or the edge of a narrow piece of plywood. Set the level and straightedge against the ceiling at several points. If the ceiling is level in all dimensions, it's also flat, so you can install the moldings tight against the ceiling. If the ceiling is not flat, mark a reference line on the walls all around

POWER MITER SAWS AND SPRUNG MOLDINGS

Sliding compound miter saws. For cutting sprung moldings, nothing beats a compound miter saw. Because they adjust on both a horizontal and vertical plane they can be set up to handle both the bevel and the miter cut without the need to use jigs or make adjustments to the table or fence. Many have positive stops for cutting standard-size crown and cove molding miters.

Power miter saw jig. Outfit your non-compound power miter saw with a simple crown molding jig that includes a fence, table and stop. Join these parts so they are square and the stop is positioned on the table so it holds the crown molding in the same relationship to the fence that the wall has with the ceiling: When resting in the jig, the flat surfaces on the back of the crown molding should be flush against the fence and the stop. Make clearance cuts in the fence for the saw blade. Screw the jig to the saw fence.

the room with the line positioned down from the low-point ceiling the same distance as the molding height (See page 137). Measure up from the reference line to the ceiling at a number of places. If the ceiling rises more than about ⅜ in. from the low point to the high point, consider shifting the reference line up ⅛ in. to ¼ in. in the ceiling's high area to avoid creating a large gap where the molding will meet the ceiling. Gaps of ¼ in. or less can be filled with wallboard joint compound after the moldings are nailed in place.

1 Typically, the first piece of crown you'll install in a room goes up on the wall opposite the entry door, and both ends butt squarely into the room corners. The adjacent pieces of molding that will fit against the ends of the first piece will be coped. Arrange the joints this way so the first piece of molding you see when you enter the room is the butted piece of two cope joints. Calculate the overall length of the first piece of molding by measuring along the wall at the ceiling from corner to corner. Do not take this measurement at or near the floor, in case the walls are not plumb. Add 1/16 in. to this measurement and mark the molding strip. A bit of extra length will bow the molding out slightly in the middle, and you can press it flat for a tight fit.

Installing crown molding

A few words to the wise: Be advised at the outset that installing crown molding is one of the more challenging trim projects you'll do. For one thing, laying out and cutting the molding will tease your reasoning skills. Since the molding tips away from the ceiling, you'll have to think in three dimensions rather than two in order to lay out and cut compound miters that join the molding strips. If you use a standard power miter saw, not a compound miter saw, you'll make the compound miter cuts with the molding situated in the saw upside down and backwards and at an angle to the fence and saw table. Needless to say, crown molding is not a good project to tackle until you are thoroughly comfortable using a miter saw. Be sure you know how to set and adjust the tool accurately for making angled cuts.

Installing crown is an exercise in measuring, positioning and nailing over your head at heights. If you are planning a large ceiling trim project, set up a makeshift scaffolding system of sawhorses and stout boards to get closer to the ceiling. Better still, rent scaffolding so you can move down the wall easily. Without some sort of scaffolding, you'll have to reposition a ladder each time you need to move more than a few feet from where you are at, which makes for tedious and inefficient work.

In order for the joints to fit tightly, you'll need to lay them out and fit them carefully, which is tough to do if you are working alone. Consider also that you'll be positioning and holding long, unwieldy strips of molding against the forces of gravity and trying to nail at

2 Cut the molding to length, using a miter saw. If you have a compound miter saw, pivot the blade about 5° to cut slight back bevels on each end of the molding. This will create a tighter fit when you install the workpiece. If your saw doesn't pivot, insert a shim beneath the trim piece, near the blade, to create the back-cut angle.

the same time. Enlist a helper to make the process easier. You'll also appreciate the convenience of using a pneumatic nail gun for fastening the molding. Pneumatic nail guns are relatively lightweight, less likely to split the wood than conventional finish nails, and you can manage a nail gun with one hand, leaving the other hand free to finesse and hold the molding steady.

With a floorplan in hand, reference lines drawn on the walls and moldings cut and prefinished, here is the procedure for laying out, fitting and nailing crown or other sprung moldings in place.

3 Fit the molding in place on the wall so the bottom edge aligns with the reference line or marks you've made on the wall. Press the molding in place and check the fit of the bottom back flat edge of the molding—it should be seated flush against the wall to create the proper spring angle. If you determined that the ceiling of the room isn't flat, the top edge of the molding may or may not rest against the ceiling at this point. Insert wood shims between the top edge of the molding and the ceiling in the gapped areas if there are gaps greater than ⅛ in. The shims will keep the top edge of the molding flat once it's nailed, and you'll cover the shims with joint compound later to hide

them. Adjust the shims so they are flush with the front edge of the molding. Fasten the molding to the wall and ceiling framing by driving nails through the flat areas of the molding that touch the wall and ceiling. Or, nail into the plywood running backer you've installed as an alternate nailing surface (See page 137). If there are shims between the top edge of the molding and the ceiling, pin them in place with nails as well. Nail from one end of the molding to the other, keeping the molding aligned with the wall reference marks. If you are using conventional finish nails, 6d or 8d should be sufficiently long for the job.

4 The second piece of molding you'll install will have a coped end to fit around the butted end of the first piece. The other end of this second strip should be square cut to prepare for making a cope joint on the third wall. Here's how to fit the second strip of molding and all others that have both a coped and butted end. As with baseboard, lay out and cut the coped end first—it's the more complicated of the two ends to fit accurately. To cut the coped edge, see page 144. Once you've cut the coped edge and adjusted the fit, find the overall length of the second molding by measuring along the second wall from the face of the first molding strip at the top or bottom to the opposite wall corner.

5 Add ¹⁄₁₆ in. to the measurement for the second piece, then mark it for cutting to length. Be sure that you transfer the measurement accurately; if you measured from the top edge of the first molding to find the length of the second molding, measure along the top edge of the second molding strip, starting at the coped edge, to mark it to length. Cross-cut the molding to make a square butt joint. Set the saw for a 5° back bevel (or insert a shim—See photo 2) before you make the cut.

Continued next page

Butted piece **Coped piece**

6 Snap the second molding strip in place, and align the bottom edge with the reference marks on the wall. Insert shims along the top edge of the molding if there are gaps, to keep the molding flat along the ceiling when you nail it. Nail the molding to the wall and ceiling as you did with the first piece, starting at the coped end. It's unnecessary to apply glue to the coped end of a cope joint, especially when the molding is sized slightly longer than necessary and the joint fits together under pressure. Continue installing trim boards in sequence around the room.

OPTION: WALLS WITH OUTSIDE CORNERS

1 As with fitting baseboard, some room layouts will have walls that meet at an outside corner. Crown and other sprung moldings wrap around these corners with compound miter joints. The ends of two moldings opposite the compound mitered ends will either be square butt joints or cope joints, depending on your layout. Cut the coped or butted end of the first molding, and check its fit against the piece before it. Then, with the molding held in place, mark the miter off the wall corner and the ceiling marks and cut the angle (See pages 146 to 149).

2 Tack the first strip of molding for the outside miter joint temporarily in place with a few nails, but leave the molding loose within about 1 ft. of the mitered end. Leaving the miter loose at this point will allow you to move the molding up or down or twist it in or out slightly for a better fit with the mitered end of the adjacent piece. Cut the piece of molding to size for the other side of the outside corner, and test-fit the outside miter joint. When the moldings meet tightly, spread wood glue on the mitered edges to help hold the joint together. Nail one strip in place, then the other, starting at the mitered end and nailing back to the coped or butted ends. For an added degree of holding power, drive a nail through one molding and across the miter joint into the other molding near the ceiling. Be sure to drill a pilot hole for the nail first to keep it from veering off course or splitting the moldings.

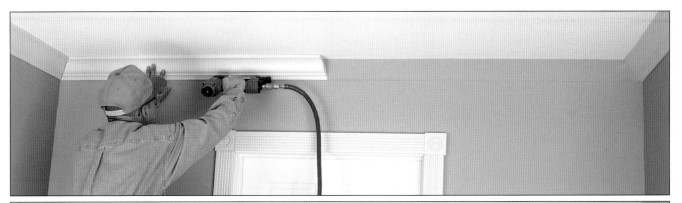

7 Install the final trim piece. It's difficult to cut and fit a single length of molding if both ends need to be coped. One way to make the process easier is to create this piece of molding from two strips rather than one. Take two lengths of molding that are longer than needed once they are combined together. Lay out and cope-cut one end of each piece to form the coped ends you need. Then, join the moldings together with a scarf joint. Cut the scarf joint the same way as you'd cut a scarf joint on flat moldings, but be sure to cut the two complementary miters for the joint with the moldings positioned upside down and backwards in the saw. Cut and nail the molding with the underlying half of the scarf joint first (top photo), then fit the other coped piece in place and mark for the overlying scarf cut. Miter-cut this second molding, spread glue on the mating surfaces of the scarf joint and nail the second molding in place (bottom photo).

How to cut double miters in sprung molding

1 Occasionally you'll have to cut sprung molding to wrap around three walls that form two outside corners. Three strips of molding are involved: two will have a compound miter on one end and inside corner joints on the other ends. The third strip of molding will have compound miters on both ends. The best way to fit these outside corners is to cut and fit the moldings for one corner, one of which will be the piece with two mitered ends. Once you have a satisfactory dry-fit for the first corner, tack the pieces temporarily in place.

2 Cut and test-fit the third molding, which will complete the other outside corner. You may have to remove the second piece of molding to adjust its fit against the third piece, which shouldn't be a problem if you've only tacked it in place. When all three moldings form tight miters, spread glue on the mating ends of both miter joints and complete the nailing.

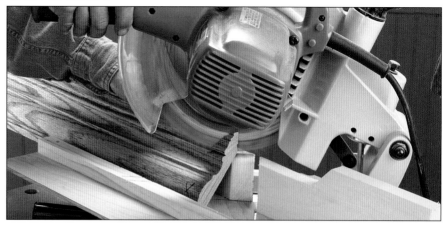

Butted piece installed

1 Start with the butted side of the cope joint already fit into the room corner and nailed to the wall. Stop nailing about 1 ft. from the corner so you'll be able to shift the butted side of the joint a little for a better fit against the coped side.

2 Set up the molding for making the miter cut. Take the piece of molding for the coped side of the joint and mark the end that will receive the miter cut for the cope. Position the molding in the miter saw with the profile facing forward and the bottom edge facing up. Adjust the molding so that the flat back edge that will touch the wall is seated flush against the saw fence. The front edge of the molding should butt against the stop you've already set up on the saw (See page 139). In this orientation, the molding should be upside down and backwards from how it will be positioned on the wall. If, for instance, the cope joint will be on the left end of the molding when it's on the wall, the end you'll miter-cut should now be on the right side of the saw. Cut the miter you'll use for exposing the cope profile on the molding. First, pivot the saw blade to 45°. One way to determine which direction to pivot the blade is to remember that the end grain you'll expose when you make the cut should face you, not the saw fence. As the molding sits in the saw now, if you are cutting the miter on the right end, pivot the blade left to 45°. If the miter cut needs to be on the left end of the molding, swing the blade to the right. Cut the miter as close as possible to the end of the molding to conserve material.

3 Cut the cope. To make cope-cutting easier, clamp the molding to a worksurface, and rub a pencil lead along the profiled edge formed by the heel of the miter cut you just made. Highlighting the edge makes it easier to see where you are sawing. Cut along the profile line with a coping saw, angling the cut as you saw to form a sharp back bevel. It's especially important to create a severe back bevel where the profile forms larger arcs, as these will be hardest to fit to the butted side of the joint. Cut just outside the profile lines to remove the mitered end grain.

4 Dry-fit the coped end against the butted piece of molding on the wall. It should fit tightly, and the bottom edge of the molding should follow the reference marks you've drawn on the wall. If small gaps form along the coped edge, improve the fit by filing or sanding away more material from the back edge of the cope. Once you've established a good fit, cut the piece to length and install it. Do not glue the coped joint. Don't forget to finish attaching the mating piece near the joint.

TROUBLESHOOTING TIP: Compensating for gaps in coped joints

No matter how carefully you cut your coped crown molding joints, it's quite likely that a couple of them won't fit together as tightly as you'd like. Don't worry. This happens all the time, even to pros. Luckily, it's not too tough to fix, as long as you've left enough extra length on the trim piece to re-cut the cope. The sequence shown here demonstrated how to re-cut a cope to compensate for a miter that has a visible gap at the top of the joint. If the gap is on the bottom, use the same procedure but reverse the directions as indicated in the photo captions.

NOTE: You can greatly limit the amount of re-cutting you'll need to do by coping a template workpiece with a 45° miter. Before making the miter cuts on your actual workpieces, test the fit with the 45° template piece. For the actual cuts, make adjustments to your cutting set-up as shown here to compensate for gaps between the template and the butted workpiece.

1 Position your freshly cut coped board (or your 45° template) so it fits against the butted trim piece already installed in the corner. If there is a visible gap in the joint, measure the thickness of the gap, making sure the new piece is aligned with the reference line for the lower edge.

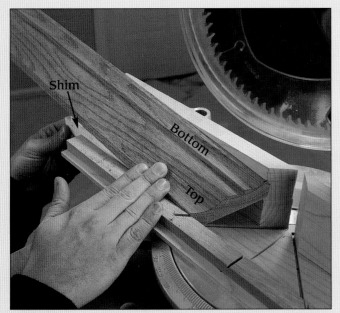

2 If the gap is at the top of the joint, position the new molding piece on the saw (upside-down) to cut a miter. Place a shim under the molding piece so the far end of the piece is raised and the end near the blade is resting on the saw table. The bottom edge should remain flush against the fence. Use the shim to raise the workpiece until the amount of material protruding into the cutting line next to the fence equals the thickness of the gap. Hold or clamp the workpiece securely and make the cut. If there is a gap at the bottom of the joint, follow the same procedure, but place the shim under the molding piece so the end nearer the blade is raised.

3 Cut the cope with a coping saw. When the end of the second piece is cut and coped, test the fit. Make small adjustments with a wood rasp or sharp knife. If the edge of one piece is only slightly proud of the other, it is best to bring it flush with a file or sandpaper, rather than re-cutting. Once the fit meets your standards, cut the other end to the required length and profile and attach the molding. You may still need to do a bit of sanding or filing of the joint.

Cutting outside miters in crown molding

Outside miters can be challenging to fit with sprung moldings because of the compound miter angle. Marking the miter angles and making the cuts isn't nearly as difficult as adjusting the fit of the two moldings on the wall so the joint closes tightly. When possible, arrange your floorplan sequence for installing the moldings so the ends of the molding opposite the outside corners are square butt joints. Cut the butted ends first, then mark and cut the compound miters for the outside corner joint.

HOW TO CUT OUTSIDE MITERS IN SPRUNG MOLDINGS

1 Mark the outside corner of the miter joint on the ceiling. To do this, hold a scrap of sprung molding against the ceiling and wall at the corner so it extends past the corner 4 to 6 in. Draw a line along the molding where the top edge meets the ceiling. Repeat this process with the molding held against the adjacent wall of the corner. The point where the two ceiling reference lines meet marks the outside corner of the miter joint. If you're not planning to paint the ceiling, apply some masking tape to the area first and draw your marks on the tape.

2 Draw a line that extends from the corner of the walls and beyond the outside corner you marked in Step 1. This line bisects the angle formed by the two walls. It's never safe to assume that the walls meet at 90°; bisecting the angle accounts for any deviation from 90° and it will help take the guesswork out of setting the saw angle. Set a bevel gauge so it matches the angle formed by one of the two layout lines in Step 1 and the bisecting line. If you've set the tool correctly, the bevel gauge should be set to some angle greater than 90°.

3 Prepare the ends of both moldings opposite the outside corner with the appropriate joinery, given your floorplan sequence. These ends should be either square butt joints or copes. Position the molding for one side of the corner joint against the wall and ceiling, and seat the far end firmly into its joint. Then, on the end with the outside corner, mark the point where the molding crosses the wall corner, as well as where it intersects the point you found in Step 1 on the ceiling. Repeat this marking process on the piece of sprung molding that will cover the other side of the corner.

Making miter cuts

As for sprung cope joints, you'll miter-cut sprung moldings in the upside-down and backwards orientation on the saw. To help keep from getting confused as you are setting up the miter angle on the saw, make an outside miter template from a short piece of scrap. Cut the ends of the template to make a left-hand and right-hand 45° compound miter. Label the ends of the template accordingly. Keep the template next to the saw when you are setting the blade pivot angle.

NOTE: If you are installing molding wider than 5 in., it may exceed the blade clearance capacity of your saw when the molding is set at an angle to the fence and blade. In this situation, you have to cut the compound miter cuts using a table saw and miter gauge or on a radial arm saw instead. A third option is to use a compound miter saw and cut the molding flat on the saw table, but to do so you'll need to calculate both the miter and bevel angles for each cut. Determining these angle settings, however, requires using several complex trigonometric equations that yield very precise measurements. The owner's manuals for compound miter saws generally provide instruction for calculating and making these cuts.

4 Cut the compound miter angles. First, transfer the bevel gauge angle you established in Step 2 to the miter saw for cutting the first compound miter. Pivot the blade left or right of center 45° to set up the cut. When pivoting the blade, remember that the end grain you'll expose when you make the cut should face the saw fence, not you. If you are making the miter cut on the left end of the molding (as it is positioned in the saw), pivot the blade to the left. Pivot the blade to the right when cutting a miter on the right end of the molding.

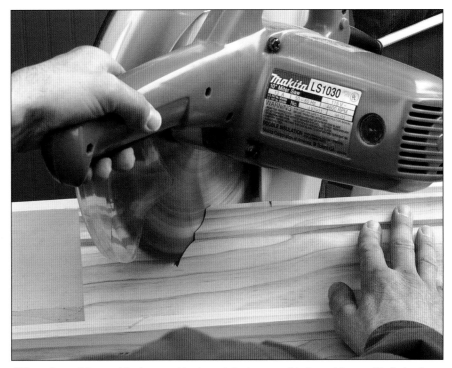

5 Set the molding upside down and backwards in the saw with the molding profile facing forward and the bottom end up. The flat area of the molding that will rest against the wall should now be flush against the saw fence, and the front edge of the molding should butt against the stop you've already set up on the saw (See page 139). Miter-cut the molding a few inches beyond your reference marks, in the waste area.

6 Measure back from the cut edge to each of the reference marks. If the distances match, realign the molding on the saw and cut to your reference marks. Unequal distances mean that the wall is out of plumb.

Shim

7 To adjust the molding in these situations, slip a shim beneath the molding on the saw table to raise the molding on one end or the other. Make additional test cuts, sliding the shim closer or further from the blade until the distances from the reference marks to the test-cut edge are equal. Hold the shim in this position, realign the molding and cut to your reference marks. Repeat this process for cutting the miter on the other molding piece.

8 Test-fit the moldings against both walls. It helps to tack one of the two pieces temporarily in place while you check the fit of the other piece.

Cleaning up miter joints

Once the glue dries, clean up any mismatches between the edges of the two moldings by burnishing them with a round, smooth metal bar. The shaft of a screwdriver or nailset works nicely. Otherwise, you can also trim the mismatched edges to fit with a file or sharp chisel, but you'll have to touch up the surface finish as well.

9 If a gap opens along the front of the miter, trim off material along the back edges of both miter cuts with a low-angle block plane to close the joint. Be patient with this fitting process and work carefully—it can take several attempts. If the profiled edges are a little mismatched along the outside corner but the joint closes without a gap, don't worry about the mismatch. It's more important that the joint has no gap.

10 Spread glue along the mitered edges and nail the moldings in place around the corner. For an added degree of holding power, drive a nail through one molding, across the miter joint and into the other molding, near the ceiling. Even if you're using a pneumatic nailer, drill a pilot hole first to keep the boards from splitting and to keep the nail on course.

Coffered ceilings introduce the appearance of exposed beams into a room, creating a dramatic gridwork of rich wood tones.

Coffered Ceiling Trim

In the preceding pages, you've just seen that crown moldings are an elegant, understated way to dress up a ceiling. If you're looking for something more dramatic, consider installing a coffered ceiling. It's a centuries-old technique that turns an otherwise flat ceiling into a gridwork of beams and recessed panels. Coffering adds visual interest to a ceiling by creating depth, but it's also a great way to introduce more trimwork into a room. For the best effect, save it for large open ceilings in the dining room, living room or kitchen. Coffered ceilings are also a nice treatment for basement living areas, provided the ceilings are high enough to allow for sufficient headroom.

Our coffered ceiling is purely decorative and serves no structural purpose. It consists of a framework of blocking and spacers that create the grid pattern and set the beam dimensions. The framework also provides nailing surfaces for the moldings and boards that make up the sides and faces of the beams. We chose to wrap the beams with oak, but any solid wood will do nicely. If you use a dark hardwood like oak, mahogany, cherry or walnut, it will lend a more formal effect. You can also dress a coffered ceiling down for more informal rooms by covering the beams with knotty cedar or pine instead. Whichever wood you choose, try to match the ceiling beams with the rest of the trim in the room.

Installing this project will involve a good deal of overhead work and some heavier lifting. You may want to rent scaffolding or create makeshift scaffolding from sawhorses and stout boards to make it easier to move around while you work. Be sure to enlist a helper to hold the parts in place while you fasten them. You might also want to consider using a pneumatic nailer rather than a hammer for this project. You'll be driving a lot of nails, and swinging a hammer overhead can be tiring work. The beam grid on the ceiling is built with long and short strips of 2 × 6 blocking. The long blocking pieces will be installed perpendicular to the ceiling joists and attach to them. The short blocking will fit in between the long blocking and fasten to the ceiling with toggle bolts. Ideally, the 2× stock you use for the long blocking pieces should be long enough to span the full length or width of the ceiling, depending on the orientation of your ceiling joists.

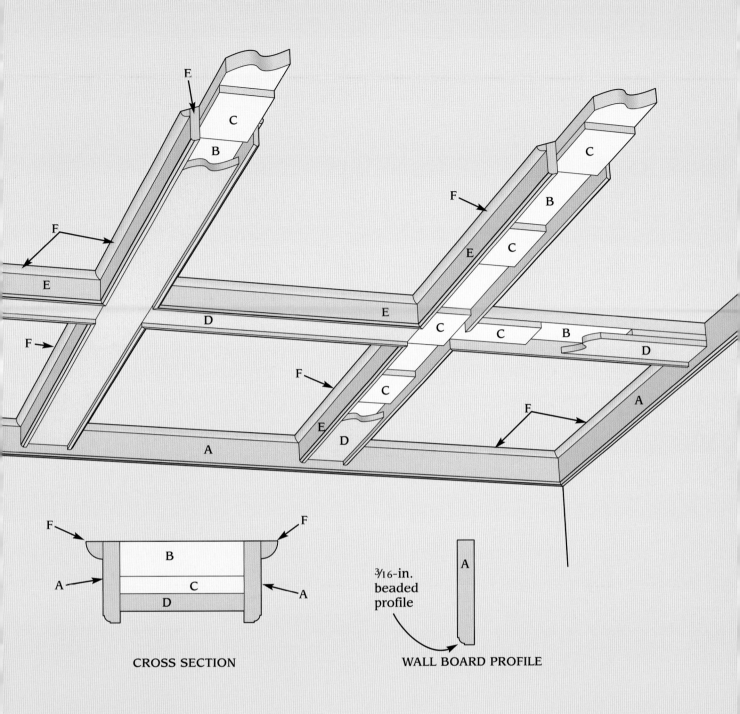

CROSS SECTION

WALL BOARD PROFILE

³⁄16-in. beaded profile

	CUTTING LIST-Coffered Ceiling		
KEY	Description	Size*	Material
A	Wall Boards	³⁄4 × 4 ½ in.	Oak
B	Blocking	1 ½ × 5 ½ in.	Pine
C	Spacers	³⁄4 × 5 ½ in.	Pine
D	Face	³⁄4 × 5 ½ in.	Oak
E	Sides	³⁄4 × 3 ½ in.	Oak
F	Quarter-round	³⁄4 × ³⁄4 in.	Oak

* Length and quantity of parts depends on individual project dimensions.

Planning a coffered ceiling layout

The first step to installing a coffered ceiling is to make a scaled drawing of your room's beam-and-panel grid pattern. Measure your walls carefully and draw the ceiling shape. Choose the largest scale that will fit the ceiling onto one sheet of paper. Then divide the ceiling shape into panels and beams. Make the beam width equal to 7 in. Size the panel areas about 3 ft. by 4 ft. or whatever size best fits your ceiling. The goal is to make all the panels the same size. If your ceiling is more rectangular than square, some panels may have to be narrower than the rest. Arrange the grid so these odd-size panels form the perimeter and are the same size as one another on opposing walls.

Another thing to keep in mind when creating your grid is that beams may interfere with the current loca- tions or operation of ceiling lights and fans. If you don't want to relocate these electrical items, be sure to account for them in the grid.

HOW TO INSTALL COFFERED CEILING TRIM

1 Rip the wall board stock to width, and rout a 3⁄16-in.-dia. beaded profile along one edge of all the boards. Sand and apply finish to these boards prior to installation. Measure each wall carefully, and crosscut the wall boards so they are about 1⁄16 in. to 1⁄8 in. longer than neces- sary. The extra length will allow the wall boards to press tightly into the room corners and snap into place. Check the ceiling for level where it meets the walls, using a long level or a level held against a board with a flat edge. If the ceiling is level all around the room, you can install the wall boards flush against the ceiling. For ceilings that drop more than 1⁄2 in. around the room, find the lowest point of the ceiling and measure down 41⁄2 in. from this low point. Draw or snap a level chalkline all around the room from this point. Use this line to align the bottom edge of the wall boards when you install them. Mark the wall stud locations around the room with strips of masking tape to prepare for nailing the wall boards. Stick the tape to the walls about 5 in. down from the ceiling so they will be visible when the wall boards are installed.

2 Fit and nail the wall boards in place, working clockwise or counterclockwise around the room. The beaded edge should face the floor. Follow the same procedure for fitting the wall boards as you would use to install baseboard (See pages 74 to 89). The first piece of wall board should have two square ends.

3 The rest of the wall boards should have a cope joint on one end and a butt joint on the other, with copes and butts fitting together at each inside room corner. Use scarf joints for joining wall board sections that must be made in more than one piece. Locate the scarf joint over a wall stud so it can be nailed securely. You may also want to break the last length of wall board with a scarf joint if the wall board requires cope joints on both ends. This will make fitting the cope joints easier. If your room has one or more walls that form outside corners, miter these joints instead. Nail the wall boards to the wall studs with pairs of 8d finish nails or 2-in. pneumatic nails.

4 Use an electronic stud finder to locate the direction and positions of the ceiling joists. Mark their centers with strips of tape on the ceiling next to one wall. Measure and cut the long blocking pieces to length so they fit easily between the wall boards on opposite walls of the room. Hold one long blocking piece against the wall at the ceiling where you marked the joist locations, and transfer these marks onto the blocking. Use this blocking piece as a template to mark the joist locations on the rest of the long blocking.

Continued next page

5 Following your grid drawing, use a tape measure to locate the positions of the long and short blocking pieces on the ceiling. Make a pair of short reference marks all around the ceiling next to the wall boards for lining up the outside edges of each piece of blocking in the grid.

6 Align the long blocking pieces with the reference marks you just drew, and fasten the blocking to the ceiling with pairs of 3½-in. deck screws driven into the joists at each joist location. Drive a pair of 2-in. deck screws at an angle through the ends of the long blocking pieces and into the wall boards to support the ends of the blocking.

7 Use the reference marks to snap chalklines across the long blocking pieces for marking the positions of the short blocking. Measure and cut the short blocking to length so the pieces fit snugly between the long blocking and the wall boards.

8 Fasten the short blocking pieces to the ceiling with toggle bolts, aligning the ends of the blocking with your reference marks and chalklines.

9 Tighten the toggle bolts to secure the blocking to the ceiling.

Continued next page

10 For extra support, drive 2-in. deck screws through the ends of the short blocking at an angle and into the long blocking.

11 Rip and cross-cut the spacer blocks to size. Cut enough spacers so you can install them every 16 to 24 in. along the long and short blocking. Plan also to install spacer blocks at the ends of the blocking where they meet the wall boards as well as at every intersection of the ceiling grid. Fasten the spacers to the blocking with 2-in. deck screws or with glue and framing nails.

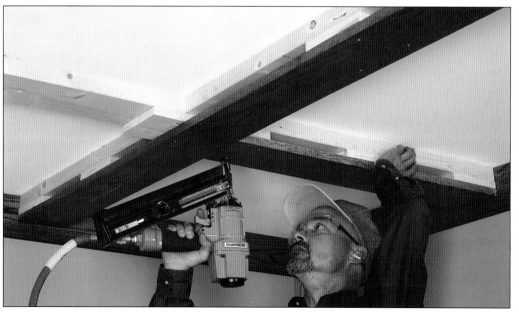

12 Rip and cross-cut stock for the face boards. Lay out single-length face boards, if possible, to cover the long blocking. (Where this isn't feasible, plan to use scarf joints for creating longer face boards from shorter boards.) Cut short, single-length face boards to cover the short blocking. Cut all the face boards slightly oversized so you can trim them for a tight fit. Sand and finish these parts now. Fit and nail the face boards to the spacer blocks with 8d finish nails or 2-in. pneumatic nails. Be systematic, attaching all of the long face boards first, followed by the short face boards.

13 Rout a 3/16-in.-dia. bead profile along one edge of all the stock you'll use for making the beam side boards. Sand and finish the side board stock now. Measure and cut the side boards to length to enclose the sides of all the beams. Miter the ends of the boards that touch other side boards, but cut square ends where the side boards meet the wall boards. Orient the cuts so the profiled edges face into the panel openings. Cut all the side boards slightly long so you can trim them for a tight fit.

14 Adjust the fit of the side boards in the panel openings as needed. Then spread glue on the mitered ends and attach the side boards to the blocking and face boards with 8d finish nails or 2-in. pneumatic nails.

15 Complete the trimwork by nailing mitered quarter-round molding around the perimeter of each panel opening at the ceiling. Sand and finish the quarter-round before installation. Use 6d finish nails or 18-gauge, 2-in. pneumatic nails to attach this molding. Drill pilot holes first if you are nailing by hand. Conceal all the nailheads with tinted wood putty.

Index